## Date Due

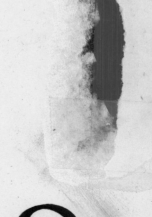

# CLASS LESSONS IN Singing

**ANNE E. PIERCE**
*State University of Iowa*
with additional suggestions by
**ESTELLE LIEBLING**
*Curtis Institute of Music*

**SILVER BURDETT COMPANY**
*New York*     *Boston*     *Chicago*     *San Francisco*

# ACKNOWLEDGMENTS

The authors and publishers wish to express their appreciation in particular to the following for their generous assistance in the preparation of this book:

For drawings and art work, Miss Mildred Kaiser, Newark, New Jersey, and Mr. George Hager, Seattle, Washington, for his cartoon, "What to Do with the Hands," published in *Musical America*, February 10, 1937.

For music, translations, and quotations:

Boosey Hawkes Belwin Inc. for "The Sailor's Life" from H. Lane Wilson's *Old English Melodies*, published by Boosey and Company, New York.

D. Appleton-Century Company, New York, for "Nina" from their *Music of the Modern World* and the reproduction of the photographs of Giovanni Sbriglia and Mathilde Marchesi from this series.

Mr. Alexander Dean, Associate Professor of Play Production, School of Fine Arts, Yale University, for the translations of "Courage" and "Faith in Spring" in his version of Schubert's *Rosamunde*, a pastoral operetta in two acts, published by Silver Burdett Company, New York.

Charles Scribner's Sons, New York, for the quotation from Edward Dickinson's, *The Education of a Music Lover*.

For photographs:

Cities Service Company for The Cities Service Revellers.

Columbia Concerts Corporation for Nelson Eddy.

The Albert Davis Collection, Brooklyn, New York, for David Bispham, Emma Calvé, Enrico Caruso, Emma Eames, Louise Homer, Lilli Lehmann, Jenny Lind, Nellie Melba, Lillian Nordica, Adelina Patti, Pol Plançon, Jean de Reszke, Schumann-Heink, and Marcella Sembrich.

Evans and Salter, New York, for Lawrence Tibbett.

Helen M. Fowles, Concert Management, New York, for the London Madrigal Group.

Haensel and Jones for Richard Crooks.

Constance Hope Associates, New York, for Lily Pons.

N.B.C. Artists Service, New York, for Gladys Swarthout.

Mrs. Herbert Witherspoon for Mr. Witherspoon

# PREFACE

It is a commonly accepted fact that a pleasing voice is a valuable asset to every individual. Everyone owes it to himself and to those with whom he is associated to express himself as effectively and pleasingly as possible. Unfortunately the voices of many Americans are strident and raucous, nasal and flat. Native critics, as well as foreign observers, with almost universal accord, have described the voice as one of the most disagreeable of our national characteristics.[1]

Usually an unpleasant quality of voice is not necessary. Unless there are serious defects in the vocal organs, every normal person can improve the quality of his voice and learn to produce sounds correctly. Improvement may be brought about through special training in singing and speaking.

In the development of the personality of students, vocal training warrants special attention during school years. Until recently it has been taught most frequently in private studios, conservatories, or colleges. In public schools, training in the better use of the voice has generally been an incidental part of choral work. In the latter case, the instructor, in many instances, has been concerned chiefly with the collective tone with which he deals or the finished interpretation of the composition. Often members of a chorus have not been instructed how to produce tone nor have they been made conscious of their own latent powers. There is noticeable growth in the expressed need for this kind of instruction, and, in the main, it should be given in the public schools where are present the large mass of America's coming citizens. Because of great numbers, private or individual lessons in such a system of education are economically impractical. Moreover, fundamental vocal training can be imparted effectively and practically in class or group instruction.

The weight of authority of educationists and psychologists has been thrown into the balance in favor of class teaching,[2] and experimentation as well has proved that students not only react favorably to the subject so taught, but make satisfying progress. In the same sense, the interest in class lessons in voice evinced by such professional organizations as the Music Teachers National Association and the Music Educators National Conference confirms in no small degree the soundness and worth of this method of teaching. For those who are unable to partake of the advantages of good private teaching or who prefer the stimulus of group instruction, the class lesson provides a satisfactory approach to vocal skill. To be sure, for those who wish professional careers, individual instruction is desirable and necessary to attain the highest development.

As in other school subjects, teachers of singing desire a manual of guidance

---

[1] Brooks, John Graham, *As Others See Us*, The Macmillan Co., N. Y., 1908.
[2] Mursell, James L., *Human Values in Music Education*, Chapter VII, Silver Burdett Company, N. Y., 1934.

which will set forth essentials and methods of instruction and give students a staff upon which to lean. Such a guide should be based on research, experimentation, and modern educational ideals and practices. To meet this need in the vocal field this book has been written. It is designed for use in class instruction in singing in senior high school or in college. It also may be found helpful by the teacher engaged in private instruction or by the director of choral organizations. It aims to provide subject matter that will give students an intelligent understanding of voice and vocal literature. Besides pointing out how to use the voice correctly in speech and song, the material is so planned as to make the singing lesson a part of a larger musical growth. Indeed, increased musicianship is a primary objective, for without a background of musical intelligence, singing is too often meaningless tonal patterns. In such instances the late Arthur Foote could honestly comment that "a singer is not a musician, but one to whom God has given a voice."

The plan followed develops specific musical and vocal abilities from the songs studied. Students are also given opportunity to apply knowledge gained from the text while they are building a standard song repertoire. The excerpts from songs used as vocalises expand familiarity with vocal compositions. These excerpts also show that the items presented and studied will be encountered in many songs. Technical expressions which might lead to confusion have been avoided in so far as possible. Finally, the lessons are so organized that progress in the art of singing may be observed readily.

Before setting down the materials found in these pages, exercises, songs, and plans of procedure were tested critically in classes of varied abilities over a period of years. They likewise were tried in individual lessons, in lessons conducted by means of radio, and in choral groups. Nor does the book rest solely upon these foundations, for authorities in voice and education were consulted. To them and the teachers who have assisted in putting to practical use these principles on how to sing, I would here express my gratitude.

To my teacher and friend, Miss Estelle Liebling, I am particularly indebted for well-directed instruction in voice, for her valuable and generous help in reading the manuscript of this book, and for the additional suggestions which appear on the following pages indicated by the asterisk (*) and concluding with the initials *E. L.*: pages viii, x, 16, 19, 61, 98, 107, 124, 157, and 164.

I hope that this book will render the study of voice — the most personal and perfect of all instruments — more purposeful, significant, and attractive to students and that it will develop their lasting interest in good music through singing.

ANNE E. PIERCE

# CONTENTS

# CONTENTS

# FOREWORD

This course is designed to cover a year's study when the class meets two or more periods a week for recitations approximately one hour in length. It may be extended over a longer period if all activities are carried out, and if supplementary material is used. Lists of such material appear at the ends of chapters and in the appendix. As in all school subjects, assignments of lessons should be specific. For example, the textual discussion of the problem involved and part of the exercises may constitute one lesson. The remainder of the exercises and a song may be given for the next period, and the third recitation may be a culmination or summation of the two which preceded. Generally, exercises and songs should be given to the entire class. However, adaptation and change according to individual needs should be made. At all times the instructor should employ judgment and ingenuity in the assignment and direction of work.

Usually during adolescence, or the high school age, voices are restricted in range and are often light and husky in quality. Because of their delicacy and instability, great care should be taken that they are never carried beyond their natural limits. Before assigning parts in ensemble singing particularly, voice tests for range and quality should be made frequently. This statement is so patent that it seems superfluous to mention it to the experienced teacher who never forces a singer in compass or power. Yet voices should not be repressed. Freedom in singing at all times and at all ages is essential to proper vocal development.

Class activity should be stressed throughout the lessons. Exercises and songs should be sung by the group as a whole and by sections of the class, as well as by individual members. When not occupied in actual singing, students should observe the work of others and be trained to give constructive comments on production of voice, tonal quality, posture, general appearance of the singer, and on the interpretation of the song. All exercises and songs should be memorized and frequently reviewed.

As an athlete usually prepares himself to meet demands imposed by going through certain preliminary "warming up" activities, so also should the singer make his voice ready for singing by performing certain tonal drills. Few lessons, however, should be devoted entirely to such work. It should be borne in mind that such material is preparation for songs and is valuable only in so far as it is applied to them.

In beginning lessons, it is suggested that sustained tonal exercises be started in the middle range of voice and carried down chromatically to the lower notes; they then may be taken from the middle to the upper notes and back again to the starting place. Such procedure insures more easily produced tones than when they are taken from the lower to the higher part of the voice. In the latter procedure, young singers are likely to use too heavy a quality. In scales and arpeggios this tendency is usually not so prevalent.

The singing lesson should be so presented as to aid in speech training. Pleasing quality of tone and clear, distinct articulation should be used in both forms of vocal utterance. Furthermore, instruction in singing to be truly productive of its greatest possibilities should serve to advance musical intelligence. General musical information and facts of a theoretical nature as they apply to the lesson at all times should be considered an important part of the building of musicianship.

* As a final admonition to the teacher for the success of the singing lesson: Be honest, be just, be unselfish, and do not teach at all unless you love to teach.

Teach from the standpoint of the pupil; adapt your method to his needs. Do not attempt to adapt the pupil to your method. Let the goal for which the pupil is striving be one which he can reach. Consider his possibilities and his limitations. Do not set the same goal for the less talented ones as you do for the more gifted. Teach the pupil from the standpoint of his individual talent and intelligence. If his vocal equipment is limited, his career will be limited in proportion.

Requirements of a teacher of singing should include an ear of the nicest precision, a refined catholicity of taste, an infinite capacity for taking trouble, and knowledge extending over the whole domain of music. *E. L.*

To the Student:

In order to realize progress toward vocal perfection, lessons should be practised regularly and faithfully. That is, perhaps, the first and most important commandment essential to attaining vocal skill. Yet it is not so much the *length* of time spent as *how* it is spent that is important. A short period of careful, thoughtful application is worth more than several hours of careless singing. You, as student, as you take up your home practices alone, should meditate upon the points brought out in the supervised class lesson: What was said about posture, intonation, quality of tone, diction, phrasing, rhythm, and the interpretation of the song? These, among other things, were undoubtedly brought to the attention of the group, later to be pondered upon by the class members as individuals. To recall and reflect will insure a better product. "Study without thought is vain," said Confucius; "thought without study is dangerous."

In beginning lessons, in particular, it is well not to practise too long at any one time. A fifteen-minute period, three or four times a day, is usually sufficient. Later it may be increased to twenty and thirty minutes. However, your teacher will advise you on this point. It is better to stand when practising singing, because standing insures a better posture.

To produce good tone, the voice should always be used easily and freely. The lips should be flexible; the jaw should be dropped naturally so that the mouth is comfortably open. The size of the opening depends upon the conformation of the mouth, but generally it should be open enough so that the teeth are separated about the width of the middle finger. As a rule, the higher the tone the wider open is the mouth. The tongue should lie well forward in the mouth with the tip near the inner surface of the lower teeth.

In singing, as in all activities, mannerisms should be avoided. The occasional use of a mirror may help you to overcome or to avoid bad habits. Sometimes singers detract from the beauty and effectiveness of their performance by unpleasant grimaces and poor carriage or posture. A pleasant expression aids in producing a pleasant tone. If facial muscles are tense or heavy, or if the forehead is wrinkled, for instance, vocal production tends to be faulty. Similarly, if the muscles or cords of the throat swell or become unduly prominent, it signifies that the voice is being used incorrectly and probably dangerously. The body should be well poised and buoyant at all times.

All singers should accustom themselves to singing without instrumental aid. To do so will encourage and develop vocal independence. However, a well-tuned piano or pitchpipe should always be available so that accuracy of intonation may be checked.

If it seems inadvisable to sing because of a cold or hoarseness, time may be spent profitably in studying exercises and songs silently, in playing them on the piano, in reading about composers, or in delving into the history of music or musical theory. Knowledge and reflection make one his craft's master.

You should memorize all exercises and songs. Various methods have been evolved to help students commit music to memory. The procedure will naturally vary with individuals. But one plan that has proved successful with many is to study the text first, then memorize the music phrase by phrase. To visualize the score as much as possible is a further aid to memory.

This book has been written in the belief that as lessons are studied, and progress guided under intelligent direction, correct use of the voice will develop. It is no less a hope that enjoyment in singing will grow and that a better understanding of music will follow. The compositions presented have been chosen because they have proved their value in helping students attain skill and musicianship. It is also believed that singing songs by the great masters or those that good taste and long usage have confirmed as a part of our musical heritage fosters this musicianship or, as we may call it, musical intelligence. No person can make marked progress in the study of singing without gaining an insight into the fundamentals of the tonal art. As a student of singing, you will, therefore, find it of value to become conversant with notation, rhythm, melody, accompaniment, form, mood, mode, and style of the composition on which engaged. By the same token, singing such standard vocal material should lead to a study of history, languages, and literature, whose kinship with music is direct and intimate. Indeed, singing is not only a goal worthy of realization in itself, but a gateway which opens into wide and enriching fields of culture.

# FOREWORD

\* To students who wish to make singing a profession, special advice is appropriate:

Be patient, be humble, and be thorough. Prepare yourself for a singing career as seriously as though you were entering any other profession. Years and years of practice are ungrudgingly given the mastery of the violin or the piano, or for the preparation of a career of physician or lawyer or architect. Yet the average singing student would like, after a few months of lessons, to be earning his living by means of his singing. The haste with which you embark upon a career is usually equalled only by the rapidity with which you return to obscurity.

Above all things, be educated men and women before you attempt to be interesting singers. A singer expresses what is in him and is back of him, as well as what is being said by the composition he is singing. You cannot be an interesting singer if you are an uninteresting person, nor can you sound like an educated singer if you are an uneducated person. *E. L.*

*Prepare thoroughly.*

# ILLUSTRATIONS

*From the painting by Maxence*       *Courtesy Braun & Cie, N.Y.*

SINGING FROM A MEDIEVAL MANUSCRIPT

# I

## SINGING

*I do but sing because I must*
*And pipe but as the linnets sing.*

— Tennyson

Singing occurs frequently in our daily lives. If you counted the times you heard it each day, the number would surprise you. In truth, until attention is directed toward it, one is oftentimes quite oblivious of it. Proof of this may be found in the fact that many of us hum or sing upon occasion without thinking what we are doing. Furthermore, in moments of abstraction, we may be in the presence of music without being consciously aware of it. Familiarity with singing, however, does not necessarily imply knowledge or understanding. Therefore it may be well, before beginning the study of voice, to ask "What is singing?" and "Of what value is it?"

Someone has defined singing as "the artistic intensification of speech brought about by modifying the power, pitch, and duration of sound." According to Webster, to sing is "to utter vocal sounds with musical inflections or melodious modulations." A simple definition is: "Singing is sustained talking on a tune." It has also been explained as "the act of expressing emotions and sentiments by using the voice as a musical instrument; it is acting of a particular kind." Or again, "singing is an emotional expression of voice with words and music."

In these definitions, reference is made to the more common form of vocal utterance, or speech, which in turn has been likened to singing. Hathaway says, "Speech at its best is spoken song." [1] That they are closely related is readily apparent. Both are produced by the same organs and, to a certain extent, in the same manner. However, in speech there is no preconceived or definite plan for delivery of sound, and, except when one speaks under great emotional excitement, the range of pitch is limited. In ordinary conversation, the rate of vocalization is comparatively rapid, and there is little difference between the stress of vowels and consonants. On the other hand, in singing, words and tones are arranged by the composer in a well-planned and orderly manner. Range of pitch is often extensive while tone is frequently sustained for a considerable length of time. Also vowels are prolonged while consonants are usually pronounced quickly.

---

[1] Hathaway, Helen, *What Your Voice Reveals*, p. 15, E. P. Dutton and Co. Inc., N. Y., 1931.

Yet, in the well-produced voice, each is the complement of the other. Speech sometimes moves into song and song into speech in such a subtle way that it is difficult to know where one ceases and the other begins. If you will listen to expressive voices, you will perceive that the two are indissolubly linked.

No doubt the person who becomes voice conscious can describe the difference between voice in speech and song and can form definitions which will be more satisfactory and meaningful to himself than any that might be set forth here, for the production of voice is an intimate and personal act. It is an expression of self. In fact, *your voice is you*. Therefore, you should make it as good an agency of expression as possible.

In considering the values of singing, we think of it at once as a means of training and developing the voice. Its benefits, however, are not confined solely to improvement in vocal quality. Because it encourages and establishes right breathing habits, it is an healthful exercise. When well done, it is a means of giving pleasure to the performer and the listener, and hence has psychological, as well as social, significance. By its very nature it has close relationship with other cultural fields, such as literature and history, and is therefore a subject of aesthetic and educational importance.

Probably no one has stated the values of singing better than William Byrd, who in 1588 wrote as follows:

> Reasons briefly set down by the author to persuade every one to learn to sing:
>
> First, it is a knowledge easily taught, and quickly learned where there is a good master and an apt scholar.
>
> Second, the exercise of singing is delightful to nature, and good to preserve the health of man.
>
> Third, it doth strengthen all parts of the breast and doth open the pipes.
>
> Fourth, it is a singular good remedy for a stuttering and stammering in the speech.
>
> Fifth, it is the best means to procure a perfect pronunciation and to make a good orator.
>
> Sixth, it is the only way to know where nature hath bestowed the benefit of a good voice; which gift is so rare, as there is not one among a thousand, that hath it; and in many, that excellent gift is lost, because they want art to express nature.
>
> Seventh, there is not any music of instruments whatsoever, comparable to that which is made of the voices of men, where the voices are good, and the same well sorted and ordered.
>
> Eighth, the better the voice is, the meeter it is to honour and serve God therewith, and the voice of man is chiefly to be employed to that end.
>
> *Omnis spiritus laudet Dominum.*
>
> Since singing is so good a thing,
> I wish all men would learn to sing.

### QUESTIONS AND ACTIVITIES

1. Give definitions of "singing" as found in this chapter.
2. Formulate your own definition of singing.
3. Compare and contrast the use of voice in song and speech.
4. By reference to a music history or encyclopedia find out who William Byrd was and what he contributed to the field of music. What was the status of music at the time he lived?
5. State William Byrd's reasons why every man should learn to sing.

# 2

## VOCAL TRAINING

*The tenor's voice is spoilt by affectation,*
*And for the bass, the beast can only bellow;*
*In fact he had no singing education,*
*An ignorant, noteless, timeless, tuneless fellow.*

— Byron

Voice has been recognized for a long time as man's chief and most effective means of expression. Before language was formed many centuries ago, the savage made known his wants and ideas by grunts, growls, and shouts. Some hold that man changed the pitch of his voice in a way to resemble melody before he could speak. And indeed this is not impossible to believe, for inflection of voice conveys meaning in an impressive and realistic manner. We know that the early sounds a baby utters, while not speech, serve to make known his needs. Similarly, much may be understood of a foreign tongue from tones employed by the speaker. Undoubtedly even at an early time, singing in some form had its place in daily life as a way of showing a common sentiment such as in war, work, and love songs, in religious chants, and in lullabies.

As civilization expanded and language grew, skill in the management of voice also advanced. Little is known of just how voices were trained and used in ancient times, but literature and other sources of information reveal that attention was early given to vocal production. References occur in the Bible, as for example in the thirty-third chapter of the Book of Ezekiel which says, "And lo, thou art unto them as a lovely song of one that hath a pleasant voice." [1] In Chronicles I, allusion is made to vocal instruction, "And Chenaniah, chief of the Levites, *was* for song; he instructed about the song because he was skilful." [2] The ancient Greeks considered the manner of speech highly important, and singing was a popular and much practiced art with them. Homer described the maidens that ministered in the Temple of Delos as having power to please those who listened to them by the sweetness of their voices and the diversity of their songs. [3] Demosthenes, the Athenian orator afflicted with an impediment in his speech, practiced speaking with pebbles in his mouth for hours at a time in order to acquire distinct articulation. In the Greek theater, a special master was employed to instruct the chorus in singing and dancing.

---

[1] Chapter 33, verse 29.
[2] Chapter 15, verse 22.
[3] Holmes, Gordon, *Vocal Physiology and Hygiene*, p. 26, J. and A. Churchill, London, 1879.

JENNY LIND

The Swedish prima donna whose tours in America may be said to have begun artist concerts as we know them today.

MATHILDE MARCHESI

Eminent teacher, of Paris, at the close of the nineteenth century

GIOVANNI SBRIGLIA

Eminent teacher of singing in the Italian style

LILLI LEHMANN

Dramatic soprano, as Isolde in Wagner's *Tristan and Isolde*

The Romans, too, were not unmindful of the value of an effective use of voice. Tiberius Gracchus is said to have kept nearby a servant who sounded a note on a pitchpipe to stimulate him when he lagged in his speech, or to bring him back to moderation if he became excited and strained his voice. Quintilian, a Roman orator, gave careful directions in his writings about the management of voice for both speakers and singers. The Emperor Nero practiced diligently to become a finished singer. For years he spoke or sang only under the direction of a teacher whom he kept in constant attendance. It is said that he sacrificed many personal comforts and almost starved himself for the sake of his voice.

Early in the Christian era a notable step was made in the progress of singing when monasteries instituted schools for training choirs. By the seventh century the famous *Schola Cantorum* was founded in Rome which standardized the training of teachers and singers throughout the Christian world. Here it required nine years to complete study which was both practical and theoretical. Through the centuries other schools of church music were established in France, Germany, Spain, England, Italy, and the Netherlands which provided opportunity for study in various phases of music. Although their purpose primarily was to perfect music in religious worship, their influence reached beyond sacred confines.

From the early Middle Ages to the Renaissance, the development of secular singing was furthered by minstrels who spread the knowledge of music among the peoples of Europe. These musicians, called *troubadours* and *trouvères* [1] in France, and *minnesingers* (love singers) and *meistersingers* (master singers) in Germany flourished for several centuries. Their songs, usually original in both words and music, were sung to instrumental accompaniment. Contests, or "tournaments of song," [2] gave opportunity to display vocal talent and no doubt served as an incentive to study.

About the year 1600 evolved opera and oratorio, as we know them today. These developments greatly promoted the art of singing. In order to prepare vocalists for careers, singing teachers came into prominence. Bovicelli, Caccini, Zacconi, Crüger, and Bacilly were some of the famous teachers of this early period whose names are familiar to us through writings that describe their methods. The ideas of these early masters were brought together by Porpora (1686–1766) who established what later was termed the "old Italian school of singing."

Following Porpora were many successful teachers, notable among them being Pacchiarotti and Francesco Saverio Garcia.

Thereafter the name Garcia figured prominently in the singing world for many years. Probably the most important member of this famous family was

---

[1] These names are derived from the verb *trobar* meaning originally "find" or "invent." See references in Grove's Dictionary.

[2] In Wagner's operas "Tannhäuser" and "The Mastersingers of Nuremberg," such competitions are reconstructed with historical accuracy.

ADELINA PATTI

Lyric soprano, as Marguerite in Gounod's *Faust*

NELLIE MELBA

Coloratura soprano, as Marguerite in Gounod's *Faust*

EMMA CALVÉ

Mezzo-soprano, as Carmen in Bizet's *Carmen*

MARCELLA SEMBRICH

Coloratura soprano, as Santuzza in Mascagni's
*Cavalleria Rusticana*

Manuel Patricio Rodriguez Garcia (1805–1906) who was renowned not only as a teacher of singing but as a scientist by his invention of the laryngoscope, an instrument for examining the interior of the larynx that is still used by medical doctors. Among Garcia's most distinguished pupils was Jenny Lind, the Norwegian soprano, the first great prima donna from Europe to concertize in America.

Other teachers who gained distinction during the nineteenth century were Mathilde Marchesi, who numbered among her pupils many of the most prominent singers of our era, as for example, Nellie Melba, Emma Eames, and Emma Calvé; Giovanni Sbriglia who trained the de Reszke brothers and Pol Plançon; Sangiovanni who taught Lillian Nordica; Lamperti who instructed Marcella Sembrich in the art of singing; and Lombardi who guided the famous tenor, Enrico Caruso. The celebrated prima donna, Adelina Patti, was a pupil of her sister Carlotta, her half-brother Barili, and Maurice Strakosch. Lilli Lehmann, the Bavarian operatic soprano, began her vocal lessons with her mother. Later she studied rôles with Wagner himself. The distinguished contralto Ernestine Schumann-Heink, who made her operatic début in 1878, studied with her mother Marietta von Le Clair and with Dr. Wüllner. Louise Homer, an eminent American contralto, was a pupil of W. L. Whitney and of her husband, the eminent composer, Sidney Homer. Many of these famous singers in the so-called "golden age of singing" became teachers when they discontinued their public careers, as for example, Jean de Reszke, Lilli Lehmann, and Marcella Sembrich. In turn their pupils today are serving to perpetuate the vocal methods and the singing traditions begun years ago.

For a long time instruction in the vocal art was given chiefly by teachers in private studios and conservatories. Gradually voice training has become a part of the curriculum of colleges and universities, thereby widening its range of usefulness. More recently voice instruction in classes has been introduced into secondary education. Although not now universally accepted as a high school subject, the number of schools considering it so have made it possible for many boys and girls to learn how to use their voices to the best advantage, hastening the day when Americans will not only sing so as to give pleasure to themselves and others, but also will speak in a pleasing and effective way.

### QUESTIONS AND ACTIVITIES

1. Support or refute the statement: "Since the beginning man has used his voice melodically."
2. Why is it logical to say that skill or management of voice increased with civilization or with man's development?
3. Give instances from early history that show man's interest in the use of his voice.
4. Briefly discuss the teaching of voice from early Christian times to the present.
5. Tell about musical activities of the medieval minstrels and point out their significance in the history of music.

6. Write a brief paper on the developments that led (about 1600) to the establishment of early opera; of the oratorio.
7. Report on a famous singer or singing teacher of the past or present.
8. Make a list of famous singers you frequently hear over the air. If possible, bring pictures of them to class and find out interesting facts about their careers, and if possible, their teachers and musical background.

MME. VIARDOT-GARCIA'S VOCALIZES FOR
COLORATURA

# 3

## THE VOCAL INSTRUMENT

*The tones of human voices are mightier than strings or brass to move the soul.*

— Klopstock

The production of voice in speech is a habit and, like most habits, is generally given little thought. Nevertheless the making of vocal sounds requires a mechanism of an intricate and highly developed character. In fact, the voice is without doubt the most efficient sound producer in existence. Since some of you may not have thought of your voice in such light, it may be well to find out what sound is, how it is made, and why we may call the voice a musical instrument.

The sensation which we call sound is the result of vibrations impinging on our eardrums, caused by air waves that progress rapidly outward from the initial vibrating medium, in much the same way that ripples circle outward from the spots where one skips a stone across the surface of a pond. If you can procure a tuning fork, you may demonstrate in a very simple and clear way how sound is made. By striking the fork, you may see the tines shake or vibrate rapidly back and forth, thus disturbing the surrounding air. The air vibrations, spreading out in all directions, impinge on your eardrums, one after the other, and thus excite the organ of hearing. Another simple illustration is to pluck a rubber band stretched from one place to another. In both cases you have acted as a stimulator by putting the sounding body or vibrator into motion which in turn has caused the air to vibrate at the same rate. The ear, however, does not detect all sounds caused by vibrating bodies, for many of them are too weak and indistinct. It is therefore necessary, in addition to the factors previously mentioned, that the vibrating waves have sufficient power to reach the ear. Strength of sound is due to the force with which it is generated and to reinforcement which is furnished by certain surrounding bodies called resonators. In a musical instrument, such, for example, as the violin, the movement of the bow across the strings sets the latter in vibration. The moving bow is the motor or stimulator and the strings are the vibrator. The resulting sound, however, would be weak and lacking its characteristic quality if it were not for the violin box with its volume of air, which, acting as a sympathetic resonator, reinforces the sound generated by the strings. In the clarinet the tone is made by a reed fluttering back and forth between the air cavity in the mouth of the player and the air cavity in the instrument.  In this case the player is the motor, the reed the vibrator, and the tube of the instrument with its column of air the resonator.

The voice, although considerably more complicated, can be illustrated in like manner.  The larynx, or voice box, located in the throat, has two elastic membranes stretched across it, which are commonly known as vocal cords. This term, however, is somewhat misleading, for it gives the impression that they are strings similar to those on the violin.  As a matter of fact, they are more like the edges of lips or delicate bands.  When the breath stream (the motor or stimulator) passes through the larynx, the vocal cords (the vibrator) may come together at the will of the player and be made to vibrate.  The sound produced is reinforced or strengthened by the cavities of the throat, nose, and mouth which form the chief resonators of the vocal instrument.

THE LARYNX AS SEEN THROUGH THE
LARYNGOSCOPE

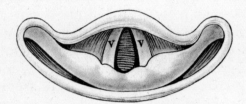

A. Showing position of vocal cords
during quiet respiration

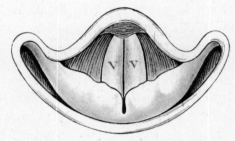

B.  Showing position of vocal cords
during production of sound

VV — VOCAL CORDS

In the human voice, as in other instruments, sounds or tones vary in loudness, pitch, and quality, according to the force with which the motor or stimulator is used, the length and thickness of the cords and the manner in which they vibrate, the length of the vibrating column of air and the way it is managed, and the size and shape of the resonators.

Although the voice has been compared to other musical instruments, it has some features which make it distinctive.  In addition to the motor, vibrator, and resonators common to all instruments, it possesses an articulator formed by the tongue, lips, palate, jaws, and teeth which make possible the formation of words.

Also, unlike the resonating chambers of other musical instruments, certain parts of the resonators of the human mechanism can be changed at will through movements of tongue, teeth, lips, jaw, and palate. Hence, a great variety of sounds is possible.

It is said that there are as many as eighty different sounds in the English language.[1] This means that, in order to form them, the vibrator, the resonators, and the articulatory organs have to be adjusted in many different ways. This should be done at an appropriate speed, in the right way, at the proper time, and in the correct order. Moreover, in order to produce clear and pleasant tones, the breath must be managed well. When one realizes that in addition to all these, the voice in singing must reproduce pitches accurately, it is apparent that to play or manipulate the vocal instrument satisfactorily and effectively requires ability and skill of no mean order.

## QUESTIONS FOR DISCUSSION

1. Why may the voice be called a musical instrument?
2. Name elements or features common to all instruments.
3. What feature is distinctive to voice?
4. Define sound and tell how it is produced.
5. Discuss the statement: "Not all sound is heard by the human ear."
6. Give characteristics of sound and tell how variations in sound are brought about in the voice.
7. Point out specifically why it requires skill to use the voice effectively in either song or speech.

---

[1] *See* Stanley, Douglas and Maxfield, J. P., *The Voice, Its Production and Reproduction*, p. 73, Pitman Publishing Corporation, N. Y., 1933.

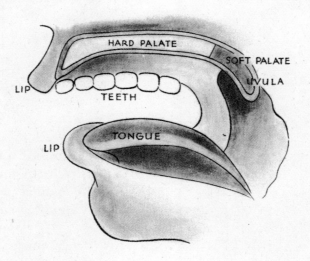

THE ARTICULATORY ORGANS

EMMA EAMES

Lyric soprano, as the Countess in
Mozart's *The Marriage of Figaro*

ERNESTINE SCHUMANN-HEINK

Contralto, as Fides in Meyerbeer's *The Prophet*

LOUISE HOMER

Contralto, as Orpheus in Gluck's
*Orpheus and Eurydice*

LILLIAN NORDICA

Dramatic soprano, as Kundry in Wagner's *Parsifal*

# 4

## BREATHING

*Thou takest away their breath; they die and return to their dust.*

— Psalms 104:29

As life is dependent upon breath, so is voice, for it is air exhaled from the lungs that sets the vocal cords into vibration, thereby generating tone. It is also breath vibrating in the resonating chambers that gives tone quality and carrying power. Therefore, if you wish to have a pleasant and effective voice, you must learn to breathe correctly.

Since breathing is an instinctive act in living, you would naturally think that it would be done spontaneously and satisfactorily in producing tone. With some persons this is true. But unfortunately, many have acquired bad habits which are evident, not only in their voices, but in their general appearance and health. To illustrate, a person who breathes in a shallow manner is generally hollow chested, lacks vitality, and speaks with a weak and colorless or monotonous tone. On the other hand, an individual may breathe deeply, have an erect carriage and alert appearance, and yet not have a pleasant voice. He may, perhaps, use breath incorrectly and thus produce tones which are husky, too intense or loud, and rasping. A pleasing, vibrant, and well-controlled voice requires a right amount of breath used in the right way.

Regardless of the manner in which you breathe, however, there must be air inhaled or taken into the body and it must be exhaled or sent out. Taking air into the body is called inhalation or inspiration; sending it out is called exhalation or expiration. These two acts are known as respiration. In repose, breathing should be done quietly and leisurely through the nose. In speaking or singing, a greater supply of air is needed and breath is taken through the mouth as well. When voice is not used, and when a person is calm and composed, inhalation is followed almost immediately by exhalation, a slight pause ensues and the operation is then repeated. When voice is used, inhalation is at times very fast and exhalation is very slow, for, in order to express ideas in speech or song, several words must often be uttered consecutively and without interruption. Sometimes one has difficulty in doing this. Possibly too small an amount of breath is inhaled, and the supply is exhausted before the end of a phrase or sentence. On the other hand, too great a quantity may be taken, and, instead of the air being emitted smoothly and steadily, it is exhaled in explosive puffs. The test of breath

**GOOD STANDING POSTURE**

Natural easy position, body well poised, abdomen in, chest high. Student producing a good vowel sound of *ah*

**POOR STANDING POSTURE**

Lifeless, sluggish, chest caved in, abdomen forward, weight off balls of feet

**GOOD SITTING POSTURE**

Body erect, back not touching chair. Note appearance of free tone production, absence of muscular strain, loose jaw

**POOR SITTING POSTURE**

Slouched against back of chair, body not poised for singing

control lies not in the ability to inhale a great amount of air, but in knowing how to use the amount one has.

Correct breathing is deep, inaudible, with no perceptible movement of the upper chest and shoulders. Singing teachers generally have defined this manner of breathing "diaphragmatic-costal." [1] The term refers to muscles that are largely responsible for proper action. The diaphragm is a large, strong muscle, shaped like a dome or inverted saucer that separates the chest from the abdomen. The costals are muscles attached to the ribs. When air is taken into the body for singing, the diaphragm should move downward and the ribs upward and outward, thus expanding or enlarging the chest from top to bottom, from side to side, and from front to back. If you place your hands at the base of your ribs, with thumbs at the back and fore-fingers at the front, and quickly draw in breath as when frightened or startled, the movement of these muscles should be evident.

To permit free action of the breathing muscles, posture must be correct. The chest should be up, the abdomen in, the ribs up from the hips, and the head and chin held naturally and comfortably erect. As a rule, the chin should form approximately a right angle with the throat. When you are standing, the knees should be straight and the weight of the body should be on the balls of the feet, which should not be placed too far apart. The hands should usually be held easily in front of you about at the waist. If you are seated when singing, the body should be forward or away from the back of the chair, and both feet should rest firmly on the floor. The body should be erect, alert, and devoid of stiffness at all times.

In singing it is necessary that you know not only how to breathe, but also where to breathe. A careful examination of music and text will always show where tone and word may be stopped appropriately for you to replenish your breath. Punctuation of sentences indicates stopping points, as do breath marks in the form of apostrophes (') that sometime appear above the staff. A curved line also is often used to show musical phrases. Rests in the music are another means of revealing breathing places. However, if you have sufficient supply, it is not necessary or desirable to take breath at every available opportunity. In fact, in some songs, even when the voice part ceases for a brief time, it is often much better to suspend or hold the breath over. [2] The phrase line is the determining consideration.

In most compositions, you should not breathe between the syllables of a word, between a noun and its modifier, nor should you divide certain groupings of words, as in a clause or a phrase. [3] If there is any doubt in your mind where breath may be taken, read the words for meaning and study the music structure.

---

[1] American Academy of Singing Teachers.

[2] The song "My Mother Bids Me Bind My Hair" by Haydn, page 166, illustrates this point well. Breath taken at every rest would be superfluous. Moreover, excessive breathing would spoil the musical effect.

[3] This rule may have to be broken in arias or songs where the composer has disregarded words for purely musical or vocal values.

It is important in taking breath that the rhythm of the song not be broken. Time for breathing should be taken from the note of departure and not from the one you are to attack.

Often a singer expends too much breath on the first tones of the phrase. Air should be wisely distributed among all tones to be sung on one breath and should flow out quietly and evenly. If thought is directed toward the final words of a phrase as the beginning word is sung, this difficulty may be avoided.

## EXERCISES

Stand erect with correct singing posture:

1. Inhale through the nose quietly and easily. With lips rounded, exhale gently through the mouth as if blowing. Keep the breath stream even. Do not let the chest drop during exhalation.
2. Inhale with lips slightly parted. Take only a comfortable amount of breath. Retain or hold breath while thinking the count of five; then exhale it with a prolonged hissing sound while thinking the count of ten.
3. Take a gentle, deep breath through nose and mouth. Gradually expend the breath while whispering distinctly *one*, *two*, *three*, and so forth. Repeat, counting aloud or singing on a pitch lying in a comfortable part of the voice. Count as far as you can with ease.
4. *Stand up straight, chest out, abdomen in, shoulders relaxed. Inhale deeply with mouth open, then quietly begin to say the alphabet. When you reach the end of the alphabet, continue saying it over again without taking any additional breath. Say as many alphabets as you can in one breath (with your chest up all the time) and gradually pull in your diaphragm and upper abdomen, — *gradually*, remember. When you have pulled it in as far as it will go, continue saying alphabets until your breath is exhausted. *Your chest should still be up.* Do not permit it to drop but continue the exercise by inhaling again very deeply as in the beginning and start to say alphabets all over again. At first perhaps you can say only one or two alphabets, but if you practice this daily for about five minutes, at the end of a few weeks you will manage to say several more, and you will have strengthened the muscles of your diaphragm and abdomen.
*E. L.*

## QUESTIONS AND ACTIVITIES

1. Why is correct breathing necessary for a correct use of voice?
2. Tell some ways in which bad breathing habits are displayed in speaking or singing.
3. Discuss the act of breathing. What terms are used to describe it?
4. Wherein does breathing for singing differ from that for ordinary speaking?
5. What terms are used by singing teachers to describe right breathing for singing? Why?
6. Give directions for, and demonstrate, correct singing posture.
7. List rules for breathing correctly in a song.
8. Indicate in the following lines where breath may be taken without destroying rhythm and meaning:

> *I think of thee my thoughts do twine and bud*
> *About thee as wild vines about a tree*
> *Put out broad leaves and soon there's nought to see*
> *Except the straggling green which hides the wood.*

> — Elizabeth Barrett Browning

# 5

## QUALITY OF VOICE

*. . . . Let me hear his voice that I may know him.*

— Socrates

Your voice is an individual possession. No one else has an instrument just like it. This is so because of its physical make-up and the way you use it. It is true also because it reflects your state of health and of mind. If you are ill and lacking in vitality, or if you have weak lungs and diseased vocal organs, the quality of your voice shows it. When you are excited, depressed, or frightened, your voice is very different from what it is when you are calm and happy. In addition, your voice oftentimes mirrors your temperament or personality. Aggressiveness, timidity, cheerfulness, seriousness, tranquility, or fretfulness beget different sounds.

Environment also plays a part, for we are influenced to a great extent by our associates and our surroundings. This is true not only of individuals but also of races. Characteristics of a language affect speech habits, and consequently voice quality. For example, the Italian language is characterized by its use of vowel sounds, and German by consonants.

Your ideal of tone is another factor. If your ear is uncritical and you do not differentiate good quality from poor, or if you are careless in the production of tone, your voice probably will not be pleasing. You may, perchance, be entirely unaware of the effect of your own voice. However, self-appraisal is desirable, indeed indispensable, for vocal improvement. Listen to yourself when speaking and singing. Is the quality pleasant? Is it musical? Listen to voices of others and learn to analyze the quality that makes them agreeable or displeasing.

Many people do not know what causes differences in vocal quality; yet they probably would have no difficulty in describing a voice according to its tonal characteristics. For instance, we often hear a voice called guttural, throaty, nasal, musical, vibrant, loud, penetrating, soft, and subdued. We think of a voice as pleasant when it is clear, mellow, rich, resonant, smooth, and well-controlled. It is unpleasant when it is hoarse, thin, hollow, monotonous, harsh, and uncontrolled.

Beauty of tone is possible only when the voice is properly used, or in other words, when good vocal habits are present. Nature gave most people at birth a vocal instrument which normally is adequate for the production of pleasing tones. It is our business to learn to play effectively upon it. If you would have

**ENRICO CARUSO**

Dramatic tenor, as Canio in Leoncavallo's *I Pagliacci* (his characterization in the aria "Vesti la giubba")

**JEAN DE RESZKE**

Lyric tenor, as Romeo in Gounod's *Romeo and Juliet*

**HERBERT WITHERSPOON**

Bass, as Gurnemanz in Wagner's *Parsifal*. (At the conclusion of his stage career Mr. Witherspoon directed opera in Chicago and became General Manager of the Metropolitan Opera in New York.)

**POL PLANÇON**

Basso-profundo, as St. Gris in Meyerbeer's *The Huguenots*

an attractive voice, you must learn to breathe correctly and to let the breath come through a free, open throat. Pliable articulatory organs are also essential. The jaw must be devoid of stiffness so that the mouth may be opened easily, the tongue should be without rigidity, while the lips should be flexible.

In a voice used correctly, quality is in agreement throughout the entire range of tones. For example, the high notes are not light and smooth while the low ones are heavy and rough. Yet it should not be thought that quality is static. It develops with practice and right vocal use and changes as do mind and body.

Beautiful tone is sometimes called *forward* to distinguish it from *throaty* tone. It is tone that may move quickly or slowly from one pitch to another with accuracy of intonation. Furthermore, good tone permits ready and clear formation of words.

*Quality of tone depends very much on the thought that is back of the sound. A tone should be colored according to the meaning of the word you are singing. Every word in every language has a color of its own: life, death; joy, sorrow; great, small; slow, fast; simple, grand. Certainly *life* should be sung with a different thought and a different color than *death*, and so with all words, especially those of emotional suggestion.

Color your words and you will color your voice, and with the changing thought there will be corresponding variety of tone color in your singing and monotony of tone will be avoided. A voice, no matter how beautiful, becomes tiresome if the sound is continually the same. *E. L.*

### EXERCISES [1]

To produce the sound of *m*, the lips should come together lightly but completely; the teeth should be separated. In exercises 1 to 3 the sound *m* should open into the vowel without stopping the tone. For *ah* the jaw should drop so that the mouth is comfortably open; the teeth should be apart; and the tongue should be quite flat with the tip near, or touching, the inner surface of the lower teeth.

*You may have difficulty in pronouncing *m* entirely with the lips without feeling an accompanying attack in the throat. If you do, say *hm*. Blow a little breath through the nose before saying *m* and it results in *hm*, thereby keeping the sound placed well forward. Thus the exercise will be *hm — ah*. *E.L.*

Exercises should be sung at a moderate or comfortable tempo.

---

[1] The Foreword to Teachers and Students (pages vii–x) should be re-read at this point.

In exercises 4 to 6, a clear incisive *s* should precede *ee*. Each sound should follow the other smoothly and without any break.

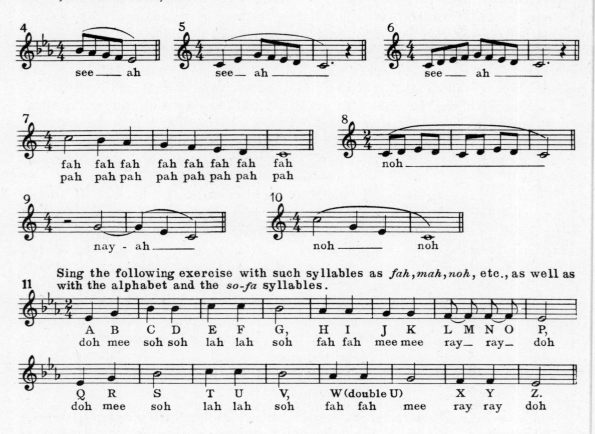

Sing the following exercise with such syllables as *fah, mah, noh*, etc., as well as with the alphabet and the *so-fa* syllables.

## QUESTIONS AND ACTIVITIES

1. Why is it said that no two voices are exactly alike?
2. Discuss factors affecting vocal quality.
3. List terms often used to describe tonal characteristics of a voice.
4. Upon what conditions does beauty of tone depend?
5. Describe the quality of voices heard about you.

# 6

## THE CHANGING VOICE

*And one man in his time plays many parts,* . . .
— Shakespeare

During the usual span of life the voice changes from time to time. The first change occurs when one passes from infancy into childhood. The next takes place when the boy and girl move into adolescence. Still another comes when the youth approaches adult life, and the final transpires in old age. These changes are due to physiological modifications which affect the vocal instrument.

Undoubtedly the most interesting phenomena occur at the beginning of youth or adolescence. Until this time voices of boys and girls, as a rule, have presented no great variation in range and quality, both being commonly known as treble or soprano. Early in the "teens," however, the vocal organs undergo marked alterations along with the general physical development. As a result, the voice becomes different in range, power, and quality. Although mutation occurs in both sexes, it is more noticeable in the boy's voice than in the girl's.

To comprehend fully what happens in the vocal mechanism to bring about these modifications would require a study of anatomy which is appropriate only in special cases and for the medical profession. However, a brief description of the larynx, a very important, if not the most important, organ in voice production, may suffice to explain somewhat the causes and effects of change at this time as well as to describe the difference between men's and women's vocal instruments.

When not making sound, the larynx, situated in the upper extremity of the trachea, is merely a part of the breathing apparatus. However, when sound is produced, it performs a specific function for which especially adapted structures are necessary. In addition to the vocal cords, these structures, in the main, are cartilages which make up its outer framework and which are joined in such a manner as to insure flexibility as well as firmness. Names of Greek origin describing their shape are applied to them. The largest is the thyroid cartilage, so-called from its resemblance to a shield. Its two main plates meet in front but are open behind and constitute the walls or sides of the voice box. Below the thyroid cartilage, and attached to it, is the cricoid cartilage. In form it looks like a seal ring with the broad part in the back and the narrow in front. Connected with both the cricoid and the thyroid cartilages are the arytenoid cartilages, so named because they somewhat resemble a ladle. Extending across the upper part of the larynx and attached to the thyroid in front and the arytenoids behind are the vocal bands. Thus it is apparent that there is close relationship among all parts. Alteration in size or position in one structure would therefore affect the others.

As a case in point, when the boy grows and develops, the thyroid cartilage pushes out, making what is commonly known as the Adam's apple. Since the vocal bands are attached to it, they too must extend. Therefore they become considerably longer than the girl's, whose larynx does not alter in the same manner. Coincident with and as a consequence of the lengthening of the cords, as well as other changes in the boy's larynx, his voice begins to drop in pitch. In accordance with the growth of the vocal mechanism this descent takes place more or less gradually. Generally in maturity, the man's voice is about an octave lower than the woman's.

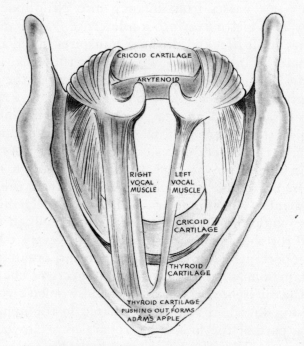

THE MUSCLES OF THE LARYNX

The voice is high or low in pitch and light or heavy in quality according to the length and thickness of the cords and the shape and size of the larynx and the resonators. As a rule, the man's larynx is not only larger than the woman's, but it is also firmer. Consequently the male voice is usually less flexible than the female.

Such, in brief, are the causes and effects of the vocal changes that begin in youth and continue until the voice reaches its full development some years later. It should be emphasized that any changing voice is, to a great extent, a new instrument which presents unfamiliar and difficult problems to its owner. This is particularly so at the beginning of adolescence. Vocal authorities differ as to the use of voice at this time. Some advocate that there should be little or no singing, especially in the case of boys. On the contrary, many believe it is psychologically and vocally beneficial for all to sing if voices are produced freely, if periods are brief, and if songs are within a limited range. Experience has shown that, under wise instruction, singing not only conserves and develops voices, but maintains and stimulates interest in music generally. Moreover, it is a wholesome means of self-expression.

### QUESTIONS AND ACTIVITIES

1. Discuss changes that occur in the vocal instrument from time to time.
2. Briefly describe the larynx.
3. What change takes place in the boy's larynx at adolescence? How does this affect his voice?
4. What are differences between men's and women's voices?
5. Why is the man's voice usually less flexible than the woman's?
6. Give reasons why one should exercise particular care in using the voice during adolescence. Specifically, what should this care be?
7. Listen to voices about you that show evidences of change and discover for yourself their characteristics.

ANTONIO SCOTTI

Baritone, as Baron Scarpia in Puccini's *La Tosca*

**LAWRENCE TIBBETT**

Baritone, as Escamillo in Bizet's *Carmen*

**LAWRENCE TIBBETT**

Baritone, as Emperor Jones in Gruenberg's *Emperor Jones*

**RICHARD CROOKS**

Lyric tenor, as Des Grieux in Massenet's *Manon*

**EZIO PINZA**

Bass baritone, as Mephistopheles in Gounod's *Faust*

# 7

## CLASSIFICATION OF VOICES

*Water and air He for the Tenor chose*
*Earth made the Bass, the Treble flame arose.*

— Cowley

As individuals are grouped into races and nationalities so are voices classified according to common traits. Two main divisions are made on the basis of sex, namely, men's and women's voices. Further classifications are made with reference to timbre [1] or tone color and, to some extent, compass or range. Men's voices from the lighter and higher to the heavier and lower are called tenor, baritone, and bass. Women's voices given in the same order are termed soprano, mezzo-soprano, and contralto. Various sub-divisions, denoting quality or style, occur under these groupings, as lyric tenor, dramatic tenor, bass-baritone, basso-cantante, basso-profundo, lyric soprano, dramatic soprano, coloratura soprano, and mezzo-contralto.

The lyric tenor voice may be described as flexible and expressive. It is well adapted to songs of a personal or lyric nature. The dramatic tenor has a more robust quality and is capable of interpreting music of greater emotional content, or compositions of an histrionic type. The baritone is of a heavier texture than the lyric tenor but lighter than the bass. The terms *cantante* (singing) and *profundo* (profound or deep) characterize bass voices. They differ from each other in flexibility and depth of tone rather than in range. The bass-baritone is a lighter voice than the real bass, but heavier than the baritone.

Descriptions given for lyric tenor and dramatic tenor apply also to lyric soprano and dramatic soprano. The mezzo-soprano, lying between the soprano and contralto, as the word "mezzo" signifies, bears the same relationship to these voices as the baritone does to the tenor and the bass. The coloratura soprano is a high, light, and extremely flexible voice of great clarity and brilliancy. The real contralto voice is rare, with deep, rich, mellow tones. The mezzo-contralto is between the contralto and the mezzo-soprano in quality and usually in range.

Adolescent voices, or those of high school age, are commonly classified as soprano, mezzo-soprano, contralto or alto, alto-tenor, tenor, baritone or bass. The alto-tenor is the changing voice of the boy. In other words, it is the boy's

---

[1] This very useful word can be given its French pronunciation or its anglicized form, "timber."

KIRSTEN FLAGSTAD

Dramatic soprano, as Brünnhilde in
Wagner's *Die Walküre*

LAURITZ MELCHIOR

Dramatic tenor, as Siegfried in
Wagner's *Götterdämmerung*

voice going from treble to the more mature quality.  It has the lower notes of the alto and the upper ones of the tenor, hence the term.  From this stage it develops, by degrees, into tenor, baritone, or bass.  Voices at this time are restricted in range, without much power, and are often husky in quality.

Range and quality inherent in a voice develop and mature with age and correct use.  Not every voice shows in youth into what group it may fall in later years.  However, this need not concern you if you are a beginning student.  Your task is to learn to use your voice correctly in both speaking and singing so that obstacles are not placed in the way of its future growth.

## QUESTIONS AND ACTIVITIES

1. What are determining factors in classifying voices?
2. Name different types or kinds of voices.
3. Describe the characteristic quality of each type.
4. Why is it often difficult to classify young voices?
5. Listen to voices about you and classify them according to the groupings given in this chapter. Do the same with voices you hear over radio and in concerts.

EDWARD JOHNSON  *Courtesy World Wide Photos*

Lyric tenor, as Pelléas in Debussy's *Pelléas and Mélisande*. (Mr. Johnson succeeded Mr. Witherspoon in 1935 as General Manager of the Metropolitan Opera Company, New York.)

THE LONDON MADRIGAL GROUP     *Courtesy Claude Harris, London*
Director: T. B. Lawrence
Modern madrigal groups sit round a table infor-
mally as was customary in Elizabethan days.

THE REVELLERS
Note the easy posture, the hands, the open mouth,
the natural, pleasant facial expression, all combining
to insure effective singing and fine platform presence.

# 8

## ENSEMBLE SINGING

*God is its author and not man, He laid*
*The keynote of all harmonies; He planned*
*All perfect combinations and He made us*
*So that we could hear and understand.*

— Brainerd

An important means of vocal training lies in ensemble or choral singing. Not only does it develop musicianship through participation, but it also may be a source of genuine pleasure. Throughout history, uniting voices in song has served to inspire and stimulate man and has been a potent medium of self-expression.

The usual combinations of voices singing together are duet (two voices), trio (three voices), quartet (four voices), sextet (six voices), octet or double quartet (eight voices), and choir, glee, or chorus (any number of voices likewise grouped as to range and quality). Combinations may be of voices of boys or men alone, of girls or women alone, or they may be of boys and girls, or men and women together. Compositions may be in unison or in two or more parts, and they may be composed in harmonic or contrapuntal forms.

When singers perform without instrumental accompaniment, they are said to sing *a cappella*, from the Italian, meaning "in chapel style." It refers to the fact that in the fifteenth and sixteenth centuries, chapels were generally not provided with accompanying instruments. Hence, the singing was unaccompanied. *A cappella* is often somewhat loosely used to designate the contrapuntal style of compositions written in this era, such as the works of Palestrina, Lassus, and the madrigalists.

Every choral conductor should train his group to sing many selections without instrumental accompaniment, or in *a cappella* style. This musicianly discipline will develop accuracy of intonation and purity of tonal blend in part-singing. In addition to training the ear and the voice, *a cappella* style broadens the singer's acquaintance with a field of choral literature which every musician should know.

Well-rounded ensemble training likewise contemplates the use of many compositions provided with piano or orchestral accompaniment. Moreover, an exclusive use of *a cappella* style often tends to take away the spontaneity and life that an accompaniment adds. For the good of voices as well as to maintain interest, the choral repertoire should include compositions of varied types. Some should be sung with accompaniment and some without. Some should be serious, sustained, sonorous, while others should be gay, lilting, and light. All should be within the comprehension and ability of the group.

Good ensemble singing implies good blending of voices. This means an agreement or unanimity in interpretation of the composition and in tonal quality and quantity. All voices should be in tune and should be freely produced. Breath should be taken at the right places in the music and in the right manner, and words should be pronounced correctly.

Each member of the chorus should put forth his best effort to help attain a high standard of singing. A single voice beginning and ending the phrase a trifle late, singing in a slightly different tempo, or pronouncing words differently from other voices mars the effect. In truth, there must be close co-operation among those who make up the organization. An individual must be willing to submerge his identity for the good of the many. In other words, those making up the chorus should think and act together as one instrument. This requires musical, mental, and physical alertness on the part of all.

Everyone should listen not only to his own, but to other voices and parts. Consideration should be given to the meaning or mood of the composition, the harmonic structure, the relation of one section or part to another, the voice leads, and the melody or melodies in the piece. Often the most important tune is given to an inner voice which the sopranos or basses may easily obscure. The conductor may indicate these and other features and strive for a unified interpretation, but each singer is responsible for his own part in achieving the desired musical result.

For effective choral singing, every voice should be assigned to the part to which it is best adapted in range and quality. Since young voices are not fully developed, they should be watched closely so that no strain is put upon them. To a great extent, each individual should assume responsibility for the welfare of his own instrument and should ask for a re-test and re-assignment any time he feels he is singing an unsuitable part. Sopranos should learn to carry an inner part as well as the usual top or melody. It broadens musical experience and makes for vocal independence and good musicianship.

Chords, both singly and successively arranged, are excellent drills to promote good blending or tuning of voices. Cadence chords found in certain compositions are useful in this connection. However, before proceeding to such combinations, each section of a chorus should be able to produce a good unison tone.[1]

---

[1] For detailed discussion of choral training and technique, consult standard textbooks.

# ENSEMBLE SINGING

## EXERCISES

Vocalizing on chord sequences serves three very essential purposes in choral training: (1) offers a means of securing pitch accuracy and tonal blend by holding each chord and listening for effects before proceeding to the next chord; (2) trains each singer in the idiomatic voice leadings for his part (This experience develops an harmonic sense and the ability to improvise correct harmony for a melody.); and (3) serves as an introduction to the study of harmony, often called the "grammar of music." A brief survey [1] of the chords usable for this purpose will show the possibilities of this type of experience.

Chords may be defined as "a combination of tones sounding simultaneously and in harmonic relation." Another definition is "any combination of tones that may be reduced to thirds." Chords may be constructed on any tone of the scale. Primary, or basic, chords are built on I (tonic), IV (sub-dominant), and V (dominant). Secondary chords are built on II (super-tonic), III (mediant), VI (sub-mediant), and VII (leading tone). In the main, in simple compositions such as hymns and chorales, the fundamental tone, or the root, of the primary chords (I, IV, V) appears in the bass. But this is not necessarily so, for inversions may also be used. That is, the third or the fifth of the triad may be used as the bass tone.

The word *cadence* refers to chords at the close of a musical section. There are several types in common use. The *authentic* cadence formed when the dominant chord is followed by the tonic; the *plagal* cadence, made by the succession of sub-dominant and tonic chords; the *complete* cadence, which consists of the sub-dominant, dominant, and tonic chords; the *half-cadence* where the tonic is followed by the dominant chord; the *deceptive* cadence where the dominant triad is followed by a chord other than the tonic (usually VI).

The strongest melodic ending of a cadence is 8–7–8, and is known as the *perfect* form of the authentic cadence. When the melodic pattern is 3–2–3 or 5–5–5, the form is said to be imperfect. In the *authentic* cadence, the dominant chord usually falls on the unaccented beat of the measure. When it falls on the accented beat, the cadence is said to have a *feminine* ending.

The following are examples of the more common cadences. Choral directors should utilize sequences in compositions being studied for an extension of this type of training.

As your teacher or a classmate plays these cadences, sing your assigned part with syllables. If four parts are available, sing them unaccompanied, holding each chord to secure balance of parts and perfect intonation before proceeding to the next chord. Practice cadences in hymns and folk songs in the same manner.

TRIADS — I II III IV V VI VII   PERFECT AUTHENTIC CADENCE — I V I   PLAGAL CADENCE — I IV I

---

[1] For a more detailed discussion of chords and cadences, see any standard book on harmony, such as *An Approach to Harmony* by McConathy, Embs, Howes, and Fouser, published by Silver Burdett Company, New York.

COMPLETE CADENCE      HALF CADENCE      DECEPTIVE CADENCE

I   IV   V   I      I   V      I   V   VI

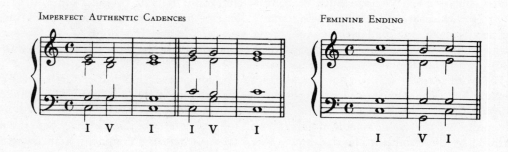

IMPERFECT AUTHENTIC CADENCES      FEMININE ENDING

I   V   I   I   V   I      I   V   I

Chord sequences should be sung in minor as well as major.

JOHN STAINER (*Three-fold Amen*)

A - men,    a - men,    a - - - men

# Now the Day is Over

S. Baring—Gould

Joseph Barnby

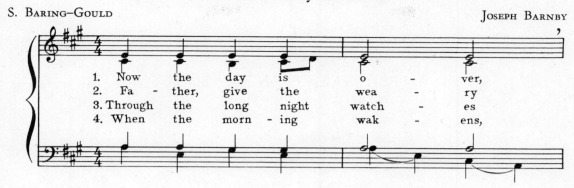

1. Now the day is o - ver,
2. Fa - ther, give the wea - ry
3. Through the long night watch - es
4. When the morn - ing wak - ens,

Night is draw - ing nigh;_____ Shad - ows of the
Calm and sweet re - pose;_____ With Thy ten -d'rest
May Thine an - gels spread_____ Their white wings a -
Then may I a - rise_____ Pure and fresh and

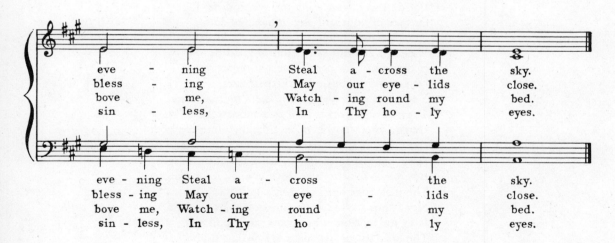

eve - ning Steal a - cross the sky.
bless - ing May our eye - lids close.
bove me, Watch - ing round my bed.
sin - less, In Thy ho - ly eyes.

eve - ning Steal a - cross the sky.
bless - ing May our eye - lids close.
bove me, Watch - ing round my bed.
sin - less, In Thy ho - ly eyes.

## QUESTIONS AND ACTIVITIES

1. Give the usual combinations of voices singing together.
2. Define the term *a cappella*.
3. Why is this style of singing good training for singers? Why should it not be used exclusively?
4. What is meant by "blending of voices" and what does it require from singers?
5. Enumerate points choralists should consider in studying or singing a composition.
6. Explain the terms "harmonic" and "contrapuntal" forms.
7. Construct a chord sequence similar to those given in this lesson for drill in blending voices.
8. Find examples of "tone blending drills" in other music books with which you are familiar.

# 9

## INTERPRETATION OF SONGS

*God sent his singers upon earth*
*With songs of sadness and of mirth,*
*That they might touch the hearts of men*
*And bring them back to heaven again.*

— Longfellow

Throughout the ages, literature abounds in references to the power of music to move and influence men. Confucius, Plato, and other philosophers of an early day recognized its power, and to Pliny is ascribed the remark that "the living voice moves men more than what they read." Poets, including Shakespeare, Tennyson, and Pope, among others, received inspiration from music and frequently paid tribute to it. For example, in "The Merchant of Venice" Shakespeare thus makes obeisance in the dialogue between Jessica and Lorenzo:

> Jessica:  I am never weary when I hear sweet music.
> Lorenzo:  The reason is your spirits are attentive,
> For do but note a wild and wanton herd,
> Or race of youthful and unhandled colts,
> Fetching mad bounds, bellowing and neighing loud
> Which is the hot condition of their blood.
> If they but hear perchance a trumpet sound
> Or any air of music touch their ears,
> You shall perceive them make a mutual stand
> Their savage eyes turned to a modest gaze
> By the sweet power of music; therefore the poet
> Did feign that Orpheus drew trees, stones and floods;
> Since nought so stockish, hard and full of rage,
> But music for the time doth change his nature.
> The man that hath no music in himself,
> Nor is not moved with concord of sweet sounds,
> Is fit for treason, stratagems, and spoils:
> The motions of his spirit are dull as night,
> And his affections dark as Erebus:
>   Let no such man be trusted.

It is obvious that, in order to have the power to "move men" by song, or to be a singer in the highest sense of the term, you should have a pleasing and well-produced voice, adequate musicianship, and a cultural education or background.

In addition, you should have the ability to interpret or express the thought and emotion in a song in such a way as to lead your listeners to a wider knowledge and a deeper understanding of the music and the text. To quote Edward Dickinson, well-known commentator on the musical art:

"Beautiful singing is not entirely poetic expression, for the voice is an instrument on which one plays for the delight of the ear. Neither is it pure tone and finished technique wholly, for without uncovering the soul that dwells in poetry it cannot move the intellect" [and the emotions].[1]

In other words, it is through an intelligent insight into both music and poetry, the technique or command of voice, the power of imagination, and your interpretative skills that you are able to reproduce a work of art which has meaning and significance.

Imagination naturally plays a highly important part in the re-creation of song. However, an imagination not properly used leads to confusion and is a hindrance rather than a help in artistic rendition. To apply the right amount in the right way requires intelligence, experience, judgment, and a sensitiveness to situations, as well as the ability to submerge oneself in the thought of the song.

Every composition carries its own message. Each should be studied carefully in order that the thought of the poet and composer may be truly expressed. To a great extent this expression will be individual, for probably no song affects two people precisely in the same way. Yet there are certain guiding principles, or underlying laws, which pertain to all songs and which should be observed by all singers. In the first place, in beginning the study of a song, the poem or words should be read to discover the meaning. It should be decided where the climax lies, what the important words are, and how they should be pronounced. The music should be examined to determine the proper tempo and to sense the general rhythm or flow. Never should any liberties be taken with these elements that will disturb true balance and real musical qualities. The song should also be considered from the standpoint of units of musical and verbal thoughts, or phrases, for, unless these are well in mind, singing is not artistic nor can it be meaningful. To maintain the correct line of the song, you should breathe at the proper time and place, so that the musical thought will not be interrupted.

Melody and accompaniment should be observed separately and in relation to each other. Although the voice part is the most important factor in a song, the accompaniment is by no means merely a crutch upon which to lean or by which to be carried along. It is well also to notice the repetition of phrases, characteristic intervals, and the form of the song as a whole, to learn the meaning of all marks and words relating to rhythm, tempo, and nuances of tone. Memorization of a song tends to produce freedom of expression according to the singer's ability and temperament, and to loosen the shackles which are a part of a lack of understand-

---

[1] Dickinson, Edward, *The Education of a Music Lover*, p. 168, Charles Scribner's Sons, New York, 1911.

ing and ignorance. Finally, in interpreting songs you should, as a singer, apply all the knowledge gained in the management of your voice to make it an ample vehicle for worthy song literature.[1]

Interpretation is not a single item in the equipment of a singer but the sum total of voice, technique, musicianship, intelligence, and personality. The ability to interpret songs successfully requires not only high musical talent, but powers of application and intensive study as well. The way may be hard, but, when you have attained the goal, untold pleasure awaits you which will repay you for any hardship and labor that you may have experienced.

## QUESTIONS AND ACTIVITIES

1. What is meant by "interpretation" in connection with singing?
2. Give Edward Dickinson's definition of beautiful singing.
3. Discuss the use of imagination in singing.
4. Why may interpretation of a song be said to be largely an individual matter?
5. State guiding principles or laws underlying the interpretation of songs.
6. Describe the means used by a singer to convey mood to his audience, such as humor, pathos, joy, fright, etc.

[1] Suggestions for interpretation have been given for all songs appearing in the course. However, pupils should supplement these, thus making direct application of skill and information they have acquired in each lesson.

DAVID BISPHAM

Bass-baritone, as Iago in Verdi's *Othello*

# IO

## STAGE DEPORTMENT

*O wad some power the giftie gie us*
*To see oursel's as ithers see us!*
*It wad frae monie a blunder free us.*

— Burns

Your effectiveness as a singer depends not only upon your voice, the manner in which you use it, and the appropriateness of your songs, but also upon your general appearance or your stage presence. Although some people seem naturally to have a good platform manner, the majority have to cultivate it.

When singing, you should put aside all detracting mannerisms and take on an air of dignity, poise, and sincerity. If you wish your audience to enjoy your selections, you must appear at ease. This does not sound particularly difficult to do, but anyone who has sung in public knows that nervousness and self-consciousness are the general state of mind. Indeed, you need to be concerned about your performance, for, unless you are, the results will never be of high order. However, you must learn not to show your concern. If you look anxious or nervous, your audience will feel so, too. On the other hand, an over-confident attitude with the air of a braggadocio is not desirable. Modesty with justifiable assurance is the ideal manner.

Practice and thought generally help in acquiring a pleasing presence. Also the more vocal skill you have, the finer your musicianship is, and the more you sing before people, the more poise and grace you will gain. In case you are nervous, it may help you to approach your work calmly and with the right attitude if you spend a few minutes breathing deeply and rhythmically before going upon the stage. It also will help you if you know exactly what to do when there.

Certain forms of manner, that have been generally accepted for platform etiquette, should be observed by the young singer. For instance, when entering or leaving the stage, the accompanist usually follows the soloist. However, a man ignores this convention if the accompanist is a woman. When you make your entrance, know the place you wish to stand and walk there alertly and easily. Your steps should be of average length adapted to your physique. Do not hurry; on the contrary, do not lag. When you have reached the proper spot (usually the curved part of the piano), stand still and stand correctly. The feet should be fairly close together, preferably with one foot somewhat in advance of

# What To Do With The Hands

**Drawings by GEORGE HAGER**

*SEVERAL SOLUTIONS FOR ONE*
*OF THE SERIOUS PROBLEMS*
*CONFRONTING ALL WHO SING*

FOUR

ONE

TWO

THREE

---

### ONE

*Cut up old stockings to supply material for hooked rugs. This will make a vibrato useful as well as ornamental. Care should be taken to avoid runs and darned places in the middle register.*

### TWO

*Sharpen pencils on narrow vowels when singing intervals expected to be one or more hexameters flat. Well placed behind the ear, the point directed backward and Westward, one such pencil may help in focusing those tones which, for the sake of a perfectly equalized scale, should seem to emanate from the spectacles of the accompanist.*

### THREE

*Tear up telephone books—particularly to be recommended for highly-strung soloists with orchestra who are tempted to strangle the conductor or toss tear bombs into the percussion.*

### FOUR

*Do card tricks or tell fortunes—dependable first aid in severe cases of coloratura. To overcome stage fright or sudden weakness due to grupetto or mesa da voce, point pathetically to the two of clubs and think soulfully of the four of diamonds.*

*(Quoted from one of at least three still unpublished books on How to Succeed Though A Singer.)*

the other. The weight of the body should be on the forward foot, or if you prefer, it may be equally distributed on the balls of both feet. Avoid moving about or shifting weight from one foot to the other, for it gives the appearance of swaying or a rocking effect. The chest should be up, the abdomen in, and the head held naturally and comfortably erect.

How to hold the hands is a problem for many singers. The usual custom is to hold them easily in front of you, approximately at the waist line. Do not raise them toward the chest, for that gives an unnatural and affected appearance. Yet you should not hold them clasped too low, for such a position gives an air of heaviness or weight. Whatever the pose, do not allow the hands to fidget. Do not clasp them or interlace the fingers tightly. To avoid such a tendency, some people hold a small card or program.

In greeting your audience, your face should reflect amiability and interest. During the song your expression should be in keeping with the mood of the composition. It is suggested that, when you are singing, you focus your eyes just over the heads of your listeners, rather than looking directly into their faces, for you are less likely to be distracted. Do not stare fixedly at one spot, nor close your eyes while singing. On the other hand, do not gaze about in a nervous, restless manner. Chorus members, of necessity, should keep their eyes on the conductor and watch his directions closely. Never look at other members of the group nor speak to a neighbor, for such actions may cause the audience to wonder what is wrong with the performance. For the same reason, the soloist should not look toward his accompanist except to give him the signal to begin the introduction of the song. This should be done quietly and inconspicuously by nodding the head. Before giving this signal, be sure your audience is ready to listen. Be attentive yourself during the introduction and interludes of the song and maintain its atmosphere until the final notes of the composition have been played.

If you intend to sing an encore, wait long enough to determine whether the applause you received is evidence of mere politeness or desire for another song. On the contrary, do not wait so long that enthusiasm wanes.

Everyone should learn to accept applause in a gracious manner. An extremely low, sweeping bow is not effective for most people, while a stiff, jerky nod of the head is awkward. If your standing position is correct, you can easily place your weight on the rear foot and slightly bend the body from the waist. At the same time, you should glance about the room so as to include everyone in your acknowledgment. Look pleased that your listeners have shown appreciation for your singing. The bow should not be made hurriedly, nor should it be made too slowly. To a great extent, its character depends upon the song it follows. However, it should always be in good taste and in keeping with your personality.

Stage deportment requires a long period of careful thought, for ease and grace of manner do not always come quickly or readily. Practice before a mirror; practice before your friends and family. Ask them to comment honestly on your appearance. Analyze their criticisms and suggestions and act upon those which are good. Simplicity and sincerity should be your watchwords. Never strive for effect. Many times a performance is spoiled by an artificial and self-conscious manner. Remember posing and affectation are far removed from real art.

### QUESTIONS AND ACTIVITIES

1. Suggest how one may help to overcome nervousness when appearing before an audience.
2. What is the custom in regard to the accompanist when entering or leaving the stage?
3. How should one usually hold his hands when singing?
4. Describe and illustrate how a singer should appear on the stage.
5. In what way does the singer indicate to the accompanist that he is ready to begin his song?
6. Why is it advisable for the performer not to look directly into the faces of his audience when singing?
7. Demonstrate how one should acknowledge applause after a song.
8. Observe the stage presence of your classmates and comment on good and poor points. Give suggestions for improvement.
9. Discuss the stage presence of some concert artist you have observed.

JOHN CHARLES THOMAS

Baritone, concert and radio artist. ("Dedication,"
page 120, used extensively as his radio signature)

# II

## VOWELS

*We are little airy creatures,*
*All of different voice and features,*
*One of us in glass is set,*
*One of us is found in jet,*
*T'other you may see in tin,*
*And the fourth a box within,*
*If the fifth you should pursue,*
*It can never fly from you.*

— Swift

All speech sounds are made by air as it is expelled through the voice box or larynx, the mouth, and the nose. If the air sets the vocal cords into vibration and passes out the mouth without obstruction or hindrance, sounds known as vowels result.

Quality, or kind of vowel, is affected by the way breath sets the vocal cords into vibration and the way it is used in the resonators above the larynx, as well as by the size and shape of the cavities through which it passes. It is apparent that sound is modified by even slight changes within the voice box and the resonators, for example, such as those brought about in the oral cavity by movement of tongue, lips, and jaw. These changes make possible the variety of vowels needed to speak any language.

Say the following words slowly and distinctly: *calm, not, past, all, care, man, fate, met, pin, girl, home, borne, cup, boot, cook.* You may perchance pronounce some of the vowels exactly like others. There are people, however, who would make a fine distinction in them. Although you may not form all the sounds possible, you should notice that those you do say are distinctive in quality and are formed in different ways. The vowel *ah* has a different color or timbre than *ee*, *oo* than *ay*, and so forth. In some sounds the lips are rounded, in others they are spread, forming a narrow opening; in some, the front of the tongue is raised toward the roof of the mouth; in others, the back of the tongue may be the highest part, or it may lie quite flat in the mouth. Sometimes the lower jaw may be dropped, so that there is considerable width between the teeth, or it may be raised so that the mouth is open only a little.

However, despite these differences, you will observe that vowels have certain characteristics in common. For all of them the vocal cords must vibrate, and the

The formation of shape of the mouth in singing depends to a large extent upon its natural conformation, the pitch sung, and the timbre or color of the sound. The following illustrations represent a normal position when vocalizing vowels on pitches lying in the middle range of voice. (*See also* page 46.)

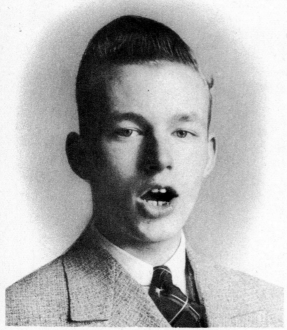

ah (as in *father*)

ay (as in *say*)

aw (as in *law*)
(this sound is a darker, more
sombre quality of *ah*.)

ee (as in *see*)
(mouth is not so open when singing on lower
middle range pitch; more like the tone produced in speaking.)

throat and mouth resonators must be unobstructed. To form them correctly the breath stream must be steady and controlled, and the tongue, lips, and jaw must be flexible. Better vowels, and therefore better voice quality, are obtained if the tip of the tongue is kept near the inner surface of the lower teeth. Notwithstanding the fact that each vowel has its distinctive quality, you should produce them in such a way that all sound as if made by the same instrument. As a rule, the mouth is more open in singing than in speaking, and the higher the pitch, the more open does it become.

You should bear in mind that the singing tone is a vowel and that its form must be sustained until the next element in the word is due. By that is meant that, if the articulatory organs move during the prolongation of sound, the quality of the vowel is altered.

Since the vowel is the main vocal element in speech and song, the voice depends largely upon it for beauty, strength, and expressiveness. Therefore it is implicit that well-sung vowels increase the resonance and musical quality of the voice. In singing, practice or vocalizing is done mainly on the sounds *ah*, *ay*, *ee*, *oh*, *oo*, often called the primary vowels, for other vowel sounds are considered modifications of them. You should, however, give thought to singing the various kinds, for all occur frequently in both song and speech.

### EXERCISES

Exercises for this lesson and those appearing in the chapter on *Quality of Voice* may be used for regular tuning or "warming up" of voices preparatory to singing other tonal drills and songs. They may be altered and supplemented from time to time as work progresses.

Directions given for singing the succession of sounds *mah* and *see-ah* should be observed.[1] When singing *n* and *l*, the tip of the tongue, not the jaw, should be active. Before forming them, the mouth should be open for the vowel which follows.

The different vowel sounds may be used in the following exercises.

---

[1] See pages 19–20.

# In the Gloaming

META ORRED

ANNIE FORTESCUE HARRISON

A ballad is a song that tells a story. The term is also applied to a song of sentimental character that has popular appeal. In the folk type of ballad, the same melody is used for all stanzas of the narrative. This style of composition is said to be in the strophic form.

The song given here is a good example of the sentimental ballad that met with general favor during the past century. Its popularity is due to its flowing, simple, and tuneful melody that expresses the sincere emotion of the poem. It is used for this lesson because the words, in the main, employ simple vowel sounds, and because the melody, extending only one tone over an octave, lies in the medium range for most voices.

The composer was the wife of Lord Arthur Hill and some of her works were well-known during the 1880's.

Observe the notation as you listen to a good recording of this song, or to your teacher or visiting soloist sing it. Notice especially the pronunciation of the vowels which should be sung clearly and smoothly. The apostrophe (') above the music indicates the best places to take breath and preserve the phrase line. When a parenthesis encloses this mark, breath should be sustained, if possible, to the end of the phrase. Notice that the phrasing of the second verse differs from the first. The genuine sentiment of the words suggests the interpretation.

In the gloam - ing oh, my dar - ling when the lights are
In the gloam - ing oh, my dar - ling, think not bit - ter -

dim and low— And the qui - et shad - ows fall - ing soft - ly
ly of me? Though I pass'd a - way in si - lence, left you

come and soft - ly go— When the winds are sob - bing
lone - ly, set you free. For my heart was crush'd with

*senza rit.* **1st verse**
*rall.* **2nd verse**

*cresc.*

faint - ly with a gen - tle un - known woe— Will you think of
long - ing, what had been could nev - er be. It was best to

*con anima*

me and love me, as you did once long a - go?
leave you thus, dear, best for you and best for me—

*cresc.*

*rall.* *cresc.*

It was best to leave you thus,_____ Best for you and best for me._____

*colla voce*

# CLASS LESSONS IN SINGING

## QUESTIONS AND ACTIVITIES

1. What are "vowel sounds" and how are they produced?
2. How is quality of vowels affected?
3. Name the so-called primary vowels.
4. List vowel sounds commonly found in the English language. Find words to illustrate their use.
5. Formulate general rules for the correct production of vowel sounds.
6. How many vowel sounds occur in the song "In the Gloaming?" Which, if any, sound predominates?
7. Define "strophic form" as used in music.

## SUPPLEMENTARY LIST OF MUSIC

Unison — Of Thee I'm Thinking, Margaretha — *Meyer-Helmund* G(b-e), Bb(d-g)[1]
S A — O Wert Thou in the Cauld Blast — *Mendelssohn*
S S A — Slumber Boat — *Gaynor*
T T B B — Stars of the Summer Night — *Woodbury*
S A T B — Sweet and Low — *Barnby*

## SINGING THE PRIMARY VOWELS (cont.)

oh (as in *go*)

oo (as in *too*)

---

[1] Throughout this book, the keys in which solo or unison editions are available will be indicated in capital letters and the range in lower case as a guide to selecting the best edition for your voice.

# 12

## DIPHTHONGS

*I thank you for your voices; thank*
*you, your most sweet voices.*

— Shakespeare

Certain words in our language require a linking or fusion of vowel sounds for pronunciation. Such combinations are known as *diphthongs* or *compound vowels*. To form them the articulatory organs move from one vowel position to another without making any articulatory break. Therefore the result is a continuous gliding tone.

Illustrations of words in which compound vowels occur are: *house, now, aisle, my, mine, boy, oil, view, news, feud, tune, beauty.* In the diphthong in *house,* the vowels *ah* and *oo* (as in *look*) are the sounds heard most prominently; in *aisle, ah* and *i* (as in *it*) are linked; in *oil, aw* (as in *awl*) and *i* (as in *it*) are pronounced; and in *view,* the vowel chamber is shaped for *i* (as in *it*) and then changed to *oo* (as in *too*). Sometimes the sounds *oh* (as in *go*) and *ay* (as in *say*) are considered diphthongs. This is so especially in words like *go, no, snow, pay, day, way,* where the vowel is long. In *oh* the sound tends to become *oo* (as in *look*) while in *ay* it approximates *i* (as in *it*).

Vowels forming diphthongs do not receive equal stress. In *ou* (in *house*), *ai* (in *aisle*), *oi* (in *oil*), *oh* (in *go*), and *ay* (in *say*) the first element is the more prominent. In *iew* (in *view*) the reverse is true. The difference in stress or emphasis, although true in both speech and song, is not so apparent in speech where the rate of utterance is more rapid. Because of the sustained quality in song, it is particularly important that the singer prolong the main element of the diphthong and pronounce the unstressed vowel lightly and quickly. It is also essential that each vowel be produced correctly and that the change from one sound to another be made smoothly and skillfully.

The division of stress, or emphasis of sound, may be indicated approximately in musical notation as follows:

mah - i (my)
nah - oo (now)
taw - i (toy)

vi - oo (view)

NELSON EDDY

Baritone, concert, screen, and radio artist

GIOVANNI MARTINELLI

Lyric tenor, opera and concert artist

LILY PONS

Coloratura soprano

GLADYS SWARTHOUT

Mezzo-soprano, as Stefano in Gounod's
*Romeo and Juliet*

# DIPHTHONGS

## EXERCISES

1. Speak and sing the following words, bearing in mind directions given for correct production of diphthongs:

my thy sigh nigh
mind find bind kind
now how vow thou
sound ground mound bound
joy toy boy coy
coil toil foil moil
few dew view hue
lute mute cute suit

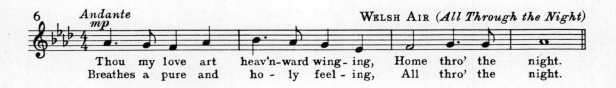

# Bendemeer's Stream

SIR THOMAS MOORE

IRISH FOLK SONG

In the poem which has been adapted to this appealing old folk melody, Thomas Moore describes the loveliness of Bendemeer's Stream. The words contain many compound vowels or diphthongs, which, in singing, should be given their proper pronunciation.

Note that the phrasing is indicated by curved lines, a method equally as suitable as the breath mark.

1. There's a bow - er of ros - es by Ben - de-meer's stream, And the night-in-gale sings round it all the day long. In the time of my child-hood 'twas like a sweet dream To

2. No, the ros - es soon with - er'd that hung o'er the wave, But some blos-soms were gath-er'd while fresh - ly they shone. And a dew was dis - till'd from their flow - ers that gave All the

sit in the ros - es and hear the birds song. That bow'r and its
fra - grance of sum - mer when sum - mer was gone. Thus mem - o - ry

*mf*

mus - ic I nev - er for - get, But oft when a - lone in the
draws from de - light e'er it dies, An es - sence that breathes of it

*f.*

bloom of the year, I think: "Is the night - in - gale sing - ing there
man - y a year, Thus bright to my soul, as 'twas then to my

*p*

yet? Are the ros - es still bright by the calm Ben - de - meer?"
eyes, Is that bow'r on the banks of the calm Ben - de - meer.

*p*

# CLASS LESSONS IN SINGING

## QUESTIONS AND ACTIVITIES

1. What is meant by the word "diphthong?"
2. Give examples of diphthongs and tell how they are produced or formed.
3. Discuss the difference in stress in the elements of different diphthongs and illustrate specifically.
4. Are diphthongs sung as they are spoken? Discuss your answer.
5. List all diphthongs found in the song "Bendemeer's Stream."
6. What, if any, diphthongs occur in the song "In the Gloaming?"
7. What is a folk song?
8. Make a brief report on the folk music of some country or people whose literature, history, or geography you may be studying or in which you may be interested.

## SUPPLEMENTARY LIST OF MUSIC

Unison — Come Down to Kew — *Deis*  D(a-c♯), F(c-e), G(d-f♯)
S A — Cradle Song — *Brahms*
S S A — Night — *Abt*
T T B B — All Through the Night — *Welsh Song*
S A T B — Silent O'Moyle — *Old Irish*

JESSICA DRAGONETTE

Lyric soprano, concert and radio artist

*Courtesy Ray Lee Jackson NBC Studio*

# 13

## CHARACTERISTICS OF VOWELS

*And when you stick on conversations burrs,*
*Don't strew your pathway with those dreadful urs.*

— Holmes

It may help you in the study of vowel sounds to know something about how they are grouped or classified by speech experts. Your attention was directed in a previous chapter to the various ways in which the oral cavity could be modified through adjustments of the articulatory organs. Their position is a basis for the phonetician's arrangement.

Listen to the quality of each vowel and observe with a mirror the shape of your lips as you say successively *oo — oh — ah — ay — ee*. In careful pronunciation, the lips usually are rounded into a small circle for *oo* which becomes larger for *oh*. For *ah* the lips are open to their edges or corners. In pronouncing the vowels *ay* and *ee*, the corners of the lips move back slightly and the aperture of the mouth narrows. Hence, *oo* and *oh* are sometimes called the rounded vowels, and *ah*, *ay*, and *ee* are designated "unrounded" vowels.[1]

Vowels are also classified as front and back sounds, according to the position of the tongue. In forming vowels, such as *ee* and *ay*, the front, or blade, of the tongue is raised toward the roof of the mouth. It is higher for *ee* than for *ay*. In the vowels, such as *oo* and *oh*, the back of the tongue is raised. It is higher for *oo* than for *oh*. For *ah*, the tongue is relatively flat in the mouth. The sounds in which the front of the tongue is the highest part are called "forward" vowels. Those in which the back of the tongue is the highest are called "back" vowels.

Vowels are also grouped on the basis of color or quality. The front vowels are termed "bright," and the back vowels are called "dark" sounds. You may more readily perceive the characteristics of brightness and darkness if you compare sounds heard in familiar words, such as *moan, main; tin, ton; team, tomb; bubble, babble; flitter, flutter; ramble, rumble; see, saw.*

Some people tend to color the voice with one quality of vowel. For instance, the *oo* quality may be prominent and carry over into all sounds, making the voice monotonous, small, and generally dull. Or *ee* may be over-used, giving the voice

---

[1] However, in singing, the lips are often said to be neutral. That is, except for slight changes brought about by dropping and raising the jaw, they may remain in practically a constant position for all vowels.

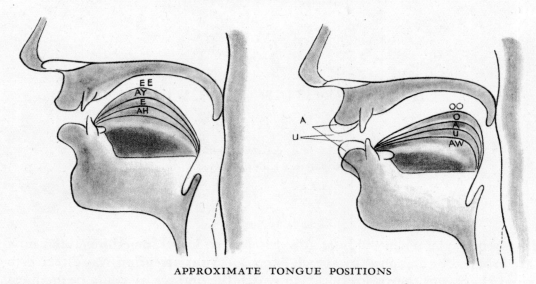

**APPROXIMATE TONGUE POSITIONS**

A. Of the sounds *ee* (as in *see*), *ay* (as in *say*), *e* (as in *met*), *ah* (as in *calm*)

B. Of the sounds *oo* (as in *too*), *oh* (as in *go*), *a* (as in *at*), *u* (as in *cup*), *aw* (as in *law*)

a metallic, shrill tone. Such habits show wrong use of the resonating column of air. Correction may require extreme measures. By that is meant that a person whose voice is overly dark should practise bright vowel sounds until a proper balance and employment of the resonating cavities are established. If the voice is too brilliant, the darker vowels should be emphasized.

With normal voices all sounds should be used. However, both speaker and singer should learn to color each vowel in different ways so that quality of tone and meaning of words will agree. For example, it is necessary at times for the vowel *ee* to partake of a somber quality. This usually can be accomplished by rounding and protruding the lips, somewhat as you do in pronouncing the umlaut *u* (ü) in German. The vowel *oo* can be brightened to a considerable degree by slightly spreading the lips.

In classifying vowels, some seem naturally to have a less pleasant quality than others, as for example, those frequently heard in *and*, *hand*, *at*, *air*, *hear*, *there*, *her*, *urge*, *are*, *war*, *far*. Some people have no difficulty in pronouncing these sounds easily and pleasingly. Others produce them in such a way as to make the voice rough and unpleasant.

Listen to your own voice as you say and sing these sounds. Is the quality as agreeable and musical as it should be? If not, observe the position of your articulatory organs. Is your tongue raised very high toward the roof of your mouth, and are your lips spread tensely when you say *at*, *can*, *man*? When you say *curl*, *war*, *fair*, is the tip of your tongue inverted toward the roof of your mouth? If so, much of the unpleasantness will be eliminated if you keep the tip of the tongue near the inner surface of your lower teeth and relax your lips and jaw.

# CHARACTERISTICS OF VOWELS

## EXERCISES

1. Speak and sing the following words. The jaw should be relaxed, teeth separated, lips flexible, tongue without tension and lying well forward in the mouth.

| err | fir | sir |
|-----|------|------|
| air | care | dare |
| war | bar | mar |
| man | can | ran |

Speak and intone the following syllables keeping them smoothly connected. The tip of the tongue should touch the inner surface of the lower teeth throughout the exercise.

mee-mair-mee-mair-mee-mair-mee-mair
fah-fair-fah-fair-fah-fair-fah-fair
bay-ber-bay-ber-bay-ber-bay-ber
poh-par-poh-par-poh-par-poh-par

In the following song excerpts, pay particular attention to production of sounds represented by *er*, *ur*, *a*, and *ai*.

SCHUBERT (*The Organ Grinder*)

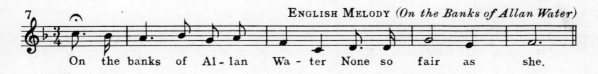

Yon - der stands a poor old hur - dy - gur - dy man,

ENGLISH MELODY (*On the Banks of Allan Water*)

On the banks of Al - lan Wa - ter None so fair as she.

BARTLET, A Book of Ayres 1606
(*Who Doth Behold My Mistress' Face*)

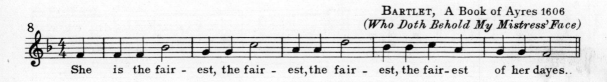

She is the fair - est, the fair - est, the fair - est, the fair - est of her dayes.

# Passing By

Anonymous Poem from
Thomas Ford's MUSIC
OF SUNDRY KINDS (1607)

EDWARD PURCELL

This composition, attributed to Edward Purcell, son of the famous Henry Purcell, is justly considered one of the most beautiful in the repertoire of English songs. The melody resembles a folk song in its simplicity and should be rendered in such style. It is typically a man's song and is sung frequently by male voices on radio and concert programs. It would be well for you to listen to such performance or to a phonograph recording of the composition as a model of pronunciation and phrasing. Adequate markings to guide your interpretation are provided in the music. In the third stanza you should notice that the words require an uneven phrasing. Sounds occurring in *fair*, *and*, *earth*, *her*, the first syllable in *passing*, and the last in *never* present trying problems in pronunciation to some singers and necessitate thoughtful production.

Because of the choice of words, as well as the intervals employed, the final phrase transposed into various keys, lying in an easy range of voice, serves as an excellent vocalise.

* *Poco piu di movimento*

by, And yet I love her till I die.
why, And yet I love her till I die.

*colla voce*

*a tempo*

3. Cu - pid is win - ged and doth

range Her coun - try, so my love doth change, But change the

earth or change the sky, Yet will I love her till I die.

*con affetto*

*mf colla voce*

## QUESTIONS AND ACTIVITIES

1. How do phoneticians, or speech experts, classify vowel sounds?
2. Group all vowels according to this plan.
3. When is it justifiable to practice one vowel sound more than another? Discuss.
4. What vowel sounds tend to have unpleasant quality in many voices? Suggest how they may be produced so as to eliminate some of these characteristics.
5. What are the prevailing moods in the following verses and what vowel sounds predominate in each?

> *Piping down the valleys wild,*
> *Piping songs of pleasant glee,*
> *On a cloud I saw a child,*
> *And he laughing said to me:*
> *' Pipe a song about a lamb!*
> *So I piped with merry cheer.*
> *'Piper, pipe that song again:'*
> *So I piped; he wept to hear.*
>
> — Blake

> *O, Mary go and call the cattle home,*
> *And call the cattle home,*
> *And call the cattle home,*
> *Across the sands o' Dee!'*
> *The western wind was wild and dark with foam,*
> *And all alone went she.*
>
> — Kingsley

> *Have you seen an apple orchard in the spring?*
> *in the spring?*
> *An English apple orchard in the spring?*
> *When the spreading trees are hoary*
> *With the wealth of promised glory,*
> *And the mavis pipes his story*
> *In the spring?*
>
> — Martin

6. Analyze the excerpts from songs in this chapter and the composition by Purcell for vowel sounds, pointing out, in particular, those which present the greatest difficulties in production to the average singer.

### SUPPLEMENTARY LIST OF MUSIC

Unison — Turn Ye to Me — *Old Scotch Air*    E (B-e)
S A — Were You There When They Crucified My Lord — *Negro Spiritual*
S S A — Ye Banks and Braes — *Scotch Melody*
T T B B — Deep River — *Negro Spiritual*
S A T B — Since First I Saw Your Face — *Ford*

# 14

## CONSONANTS

*His words were simple words enough,*
*And yet he used them so,*
*That what in other mouths was rough,*
*In his seemed musical and low.*

— Lowell

In speech, when the escaping breath stream meets with an obstruction formed by the tongue, lips, teeth, or velum (soft palate), the resulting sound is called a *consonant*. The word comes from the Latin, *con* and *sonare*, meaning "with sound" or "to sound together." The dictionary defines it as "an articulate sound characterized by friction, squeezing, or stopping of the breath in some part of the mouth. It is usually sounded with a more open sound called a vowel." In other words, a consonant is formed when the vowel chamber is blocked either partially or wholly.

As there are many vowel sounds possible through adjustments of the articulatory organs, so also can many consonants be formed by making the blockage in different ways. Say slowly the following words, paying careful attention to the quality of consonants and the manner in which you produce them: *to, do, pay, bee, key, go, lay, may, no, hang, red, vow, foe, see, rise, who, we, how, you, jug, chew, she, measure, thing, though*. No doubt you noticed that, in order to pronounce some consonants, the column of air was at times completely stopped by the organs of speech and then released with a sudden explosion or puff; or sometimes it was only partially stopped, thus allowing the breath to escape gradually. When the current of air is completely stopped and then released suddenly, sounds produced are called *stop consonants* or *explosives*. They occur in the sounds *t* in *to*, *d* in *do*, *p* in *pay*, *b* in *be*, *k* in *key*, *g* in *go*, *j* in *jug*, and *ch* in *chin*. When the breath stream is only partly blocked, as in the sounds represented by *r, l, m, n, ng, th, f, v, s, z, y, sh*, consonants called *continuants* are formed. Stop, or explosive consonants, are uttered quickly, but continuants may be lengthened or sounded continuously as the word implies.

In producing some consonants, the tip of the tongue obstructs the stream of breath; in others, the teeth and lips hinder the free emission of air, and sometimes the back of the tongue forms the blockage. Consonants articulated by the two lips (as *p, b, m*) are called *bi-labial* sounds; those formed by the lower lip against the upper teeth (as *f*, *v*) are known as labio-dental sounds. Those produced by the tip or blade of the tongue against the teeth or teeth-ridge (as *t*, *d*, *n*, *th*) are classified as dental sounds. Sounds articulated by the front of the tongue against the hard palate are termed palatal (as *y*), and those made by the back of the tongue against the soft palate (as *k*, *g*, and *ng*) are called velar sounds. In most sounds, breath escapes through the oral cavity or mouth. However, in *m*, *n*, and *ng* air is released through the nose. For this reason, these sounds are often called nasal or resonant consonants.

In some consonants, the vocal cords vibrate, making *voiced* sounds. In others they do not and the consonants are said to be *voiceless* or *breathed*. Voiced and voiceless consonants generally are in pairs. For example, *b* (as in *bin*) represents a voiced sound of which *p* (as in *pin*) is the voiceless equivalent. The sound *d* (as in *din*) is voiced; *t* (as in *tin*) is voiceless. The sound *v* (as in *vie*) is voiced, but *f* (as in *fie*) is voiceless. In the word *this*, the first sound (*th*) is voiced; yet in the word *thin* it is voiceless. In the final sound in *rose*, the vocal cords vibrate but in *house* they do not. The medial consonant in *pleasure* is voiced, and its voiceless equivalent is found in the initial sound in *she*. In the beginning sound in *we*, voice is present, while in *why* it is absent. The aspirate sound represented by the letter *h* has no voiced counterpart, nor do *m*, *n*, *ng*, *r*, and *l* have voiceless forms.

The sounds *w* in *we* and *y* in *you* are often called semi-vowels, for, in their production, friction is practically imperceptible. They are also sometimes defined as vowels used in the capacity of consonants. The continuant consonants *l*, *m*, and *n* also are classified as semi-vowels, for they frequently constitute syllables by themselves without accompanying vowels; as, for example, *little*, *prism*, *heav'n*.

The sound represented by the symbol *r* is generally considered a consonant, but in certain words it becomes part of the vowel (as in *air*, *far*, *err*). Some people omit or "drop" *r* when it is final in a word (as in *ever*, *far*), or when it comes before a consonant (as in *bird*, *harm*). But final *r*, if followed by a word beginning with a vowel (as *far away*), should be lightly trilled or rolled[1] in singing. To insure better quality and to give it greater clarity or distinctness, *r* also should be lightly trilled when it is the initial consonant (as in *rose*), when it occurs between two vowels (as in *sorrow*), and when it is used with other consonants (as in *three*).

Although vowels are the chief vocal element in speaking and singing, it is the consonant that gives them character and meaning. To cite specifically, the vowels in *see*, *bee*, *tree*, *me*, *seed*, *heed* are the same, but the consonants used with them entirely change the sense of the word. It is obvious, therefore, that, if you wish to speak and sing effectively, you must learn to produce consonants accurately and skillfully. It is well in forming them to keep the tip of the tongue well for-

---

[1] The singer should avoid a heavily trilled or exaggerated roll in producing this sound.

ward in the mouth. There is often a tendency to retract or invert it, particularly in *r* and *l*, which gives these and surrounding sounds an unpleasant quality.

\* There is an old rule for speech which is helpful in singing: "Be sparing [merciful] with the vowels and you will speak beautifully; honor the consonants and you will speak distinctly."

*Honor the consonants.* There are twenty-one of them in our alphabet and only five vowels, so they must be important to speech. They give it meaning; they color your singing. Sing on or stress the consonants when it helps to make your enunciation of a word more interesting. For instance, if you say 'won-derful', and pause for an instant on the *n*, it really sounds more wonderful than if you say 'wo-nderful', and stress the vowel. If you say 'whis-pering', and accent the *s* just a little, it really sounds like a whisper.

Learn to look for the consonant in a word that will help to make the word more interesting and give it meaning, and then sing on it. *E. L.*

EXERCISES

Substitute other consonants as *b, p, d, t, n, m, l.*
The vowel sound may be changed also.

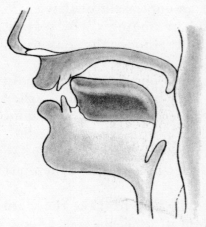

A. For dental consonants (such as *t, d*)

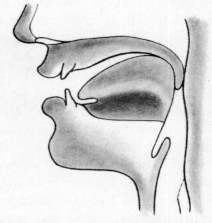

B. For velar consonants (such as *k, g*)

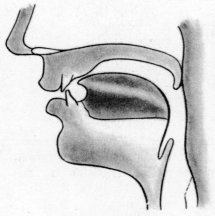

C. For *s* and *z*

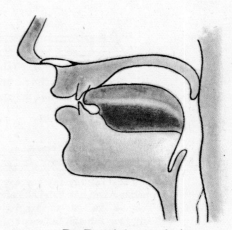

D. For *th* (as in *thin*)

## TABLE OF CONSONANTS

| Stoppage or friction made by | Lips | | Lower lip and upper teeth | | Teeth, or teeth ridge, and tongue | | Palate and tongue | Velum and tongue | | Glottis |
|---|---|---|---|---|---|---|---|---|---|---|
| Kind of sound | o voiceless | — voiced | o | — | o | — | — | o | — | o |
| Plosive | p | b | | | t ch | d j | | k | g | |
| Continuant (Fricative) | wh | w | f | v | th[1] s sh | l th[2] z ʒ[3] | y | | | h (aspirate sound) |
| Nasal | | m | | | | n | | | ng | |
| Rolled (or trilled) | | | | | | r | | | | |

[1] *th* as in *thin*     [2] *th* as in *this*     [3] ʒ as in *azure*

# Wandering

FRANZ SCHUBERT
(1797–1828)

Schubert, one of the greatest of all song writers, spent most of his brief life in poverty and obscurity. Not until after his death was his genius generally recognized. He wrote nine symphonies, a considerable amount of chamber music, piano pieces, operas, masses, and other choral works. But his songs, of which he composed over 600, were his greatest contribution to music. He was the originator of the "art song" which is often spoken of as the most characteristic innovation of the Romantic Period in music.

Schubert's "Wandering" is the opening song in "The Mill Cycle." The poem, by Wilhelm Müller, tells the story of a miller's charming daughter who was loved by her father's apprentice. At first she apparently loved him in return, but later she transferred her affections to a gay young huntsman. The first songs tell about the mill, the brook, and the young miller's wooing. After the huntsman made his appearance, despair settled upon the apprentice. When convinced he had lost his sweetheart forever, he drowned himself in the brook, which in the last number of the group, sings a lullaby to him.

In "Wandering" the young miller describes his delight in travel. It leads effectively into the next song of the cycle where he approaches the home of the young maiden with whom he later fell in love. The broken chords in the right hand of the accompaniment and the repeated octaves in the left depict the sprightly movement of the brook as it turns the mill wheel. The melody is as simple and direct as any folk tune and should be sung in such manner.

The correct tempo is fairly rapid, requiring clear, crisp enunciation of the text.

must    a wretch-ed    mill-er be,    Who nev - er cares the    world to see, To
knows    no rest    by    day or night,    In—wand-'ring    al - ways    takes de-light, The

wan - der, to— wan - der, to    wan - der, to— wan - der.
wa - ter, the wa - ter, the    wa - ter, the wa - ter.

*pp*

3. We
4. The
5. To

see    it    in the    mill - wheels too,    The    mill - wheels,    We
ver - y stones for    all— their weight,    The    mill - stones,    The
wan - der far - ther    I— de - sire,    To    wan - der,    To

see it in the mill-wheels too, The mill - wheels, They
ver - y stones for all_ their weight, The mill - stones, Keep
wan-der far - ther I_ de - sire, To wan - der, O_

like not to be stand-ing_ still, But turn all day with right good-will, The
danc-ing in the mer - ry_round, And will not be in - ac - tive found, The
Mas - ter, and O Mis - tress too, Let me in peace de - part from you, And

mill - wheels, the mill - wheels, the mill - wheels, the mill - wheels.
mill - stones, the mill - stones, the mill - stones, the mill - stones.
wan - der, and wan - der, and wan - der, and wan - der.

V. 3. & 4. V. 5.

# CLASS LESSONS IN SINGING

## QUESTIONS AND ACTIVITIES

1. What are consonants and how are they produced?
2. Compare and contrast consonants with vowels.
3. What is meant by "voiced" and "voiceless" consonants? Give specific examples of each type.
4. Tell what the following terms mean when used in connection with formation of consonants: explosive; nasal; continuant. Give definite illustrations of each.
5. List consonants found in the English language according to the manner in which they are produced or formed by the articulatory organs.
6. Why is it important that consonants be clearly and distinctly uttered in both speech and song?
7. Formulate rules for production of consonants in singing.
8. Analyze the song "Wandering" for consonants. How many kinds occur? Which are used most?
9. Read about Franz Schubert in Grove's *Dictionary of Music* or in one of the various biographies. Write a brief sketch of his life, noting the titles of his works which have become world favorites. List the names of his compositions which you have heard on solo artist, orchestral, and radio programs.

## SUPPLEMENTARY LIST OF MUSIC

Unison — The Lass of Richmond Hill — *Hook.* Bb(c-eb)
S A — Country Gardens — *Old English*, arr. by *Treharne*
S S A — O Dear What Can the Matter Be — *Old English*, arr. by *Grant-Schaefer*
T T B B — Tell Me Not of a Lovely Lass — *Forsyth*
S A T B — Matona, Lovely Maiden — *Lassus*

ROSE BAMPTON

Mezzo-soprano, oratorio and concert artist

*Courtesy Herbert Mitchell*

# 15

## COMBINATIONS OF CONSONANTS

*Once more, speak clearly*
*If you speak at all,*
*Carve every word*
*Before you let it fall.*

— Holmes

Consonants, like vowels, often appear in combination. If you select a book at random, a cursory glance of even a few lines will show many different groupings. For example, in the following words one consonant sound must quickly follow another for correct pronunciation: *still, splendid, blast, strand, thread, clamp, church, grudge, Scotch, splinter, sprinkling, stumble.*

But separate sounds are not always formed when two letters representing consonants appear together. Although two such symbols are combined in *the, who, she, thing,* only one sound is made. Conversely, a single letter may represent more than one sound. In producing the consonant *x* in *axe,* the sounds *k* and *s* are made; in *exact, g* and *z* are formed. According to some speech experts, a compound consonant is heard in *gem, jet, jug, huge.* They believe that, in order to pronounce *g* and *j* in these words, the tongue moves quickly from *d* to that for *z* (as in *azure*).

To utter such succession of sounds acceptably requires quick adjustment of the articulatory organs. Tongue, lips, and jaw must be flexible and readily responsive to demands placed upon them.

EXERCISES (continued on page 72.)

1. brah bray bree broh broo
   flah flay flee floh floo
   Use other consonant combinations
   as: *tr, str, pl, gr,* etc.

2. brah bray bree broh broo
   flah flay flee floh floo
   Lightly trill or roll the **r** sound.

BRAHMS (*The Sandman*)

3. Sleep— on! Sleep— on,— sleep on my— lit-tle one. —

# Have You Seen But a White Lily Grow

BEN JONSON

MUSIC ANONYMOUS
(1614)

Ben Jonson (1573–1634) was one of the foremost literary men of that golden age of English literature. By some he is credited with being the most learned poet of his time. His plays reveal careful study and research, but are heavy, long, and of little interest today. On the contrary, his lyrics exhibit spontaneity and charm and are gems of poetic grace. These qualities are found in the present selection. The old English melody of anonymous origin matches it admirably in simplicity and beauty.

Study the text carefully, noting the pronunciation of the unusual old English words. Extract the ascending scale of D major and practice it for evenness of tone. Trill the "r" in "grow" on eighth note *d* and continue up the scale on the sound of long "o."

Have you seen but a white li-ly grow___ be-fore rude hands had touch'd it; Have you mark'd__ but the fall of the snow be-fore the earth__ hath smutch'd it, Have you felt the wool of bea-ver,

Or swan's down ev-er, Or have smelt of the bud of the bri-er,

Or the nard in the fire, Or have tast-ed the bag of the

bee; Oh so white, Oh so soft, Oh so sweet, so sweet, So sweet is

she! Oh so white, Oh so soft, Oh so sweet, so sweet, so sweet is she!

# Loch Lomond

SCOTCH AIR

This is one of the most familiar and best loved of old Scotch folk songs. The melody is constructed on a scale line which avoids the fourth and the seventh tones, and is a good example of what is known as the pentatonic or five-tone scale, expressed 1–2–3–5–6, with 8 making a six-tone scale from *do* to *do*, *i.e.* tonic to tonic.

It is said that the words refer to a political exile who will return to his native land only in spirit. Loch Lomond, one of the most beautiful lakes in Scotland, is a few miles northwest of Glasgow.

The sixteenth note, followed by a dotted eighth, (the reverse of the usual long note followed by the dotted note) is characteristic of the music of Scotland, and is known as the "Scotch snap." It should be sung quickly but without distortion to the rhythmic flow of the phrase.

1. By —— yon bon - nie banks and by yon bon - nie braes, Where the
2. 'Twas —— there that we part - ed in yon sha - dy glen, On the
3. The —— wee bird - ies sing and the wild flow - ers spring, And in

sun shines bright on Loch Lo - mond, Where I and my true love were
steep, steep side of Ben Lo - mond, Where in pur - ple hue —— the
sun - shine the wa - ters are sleep - ing, But the bro - ken heart it kens —— nae

ev - er wont to gae, On the bon-nie, bon-nie banks of Loch Lo - mond.
High-land hills we view, And the moon com-ing out in the gloam - ing.
sec - ond spring a - gain, Tho' the wae - fu' may cease frae their greet - ing.

REFRAIN

Oh! ye'll tak' the high road, and I'll tak' the low road, And

I'll be in Scot - land a - fore ye; But I and my true love we'll

nev - er meet a - gain, On the bon-nie, bon-nie banks of Loch Lo - mond. —

*(Oft in the Stilly Night)*

Oft in the stil - ly night, Ere slum - ber's chain has bound ___ me

Fond mem - 'ry brings the light Of oth - er days a - round me.

## QUESTIONS AND ACTIVITIES

1. What articulatory adjustments are necessary to pronounce the following combination of consonants: *br; pl; str; thr; gl; spl; fl.*
2. Make a list of at least ten words that contain groups of consonants in the same syllable that must be enunciated quickly.
3. Find at least five words that have double consonant sounds, but are represented by only one symbol.
4. Analyze the songs "Have You Seen But a White Lily Grow?" and "Loch Lomond" for different combinations of consonants.
5. With what works by Ben Jonson are you familiar?
6. Write a brief paper on the music of England during the reign of Queen Elizabeth.
7. Report on the Grove's Dictionary references to Pentatonic Scale, Hexachord, and Scotch Snap.

## SUPPLEMENTARY LIST OF MUSIC

Unison — My Love's an Arbutus — *Irish Air.* Ab(eb-f), G(d-e), F(c-d)
S A — The Little Dustman — *Brahms*
S S A — The Water Lily — *Abt*
T T B B — Lo, How a Rose E'er Blooming — *Praetorius*
S A T B — Ye Watchers and Ye Holy Ones — *German Melody*, arr. by *Fischer*

# 16

## PRONUNCIATION

*. . . words once spoke can never be recalled.*

— Dillon

Pronunciation of English, like other languages, is subject to change from time to time and from place to place. If you listen to elderly people converse, you may find that many of them often pronounce words quite differently from current usage. Also, if you travel in different sections of the country, you will hear different pronunciations as well as different idioms. To illustrate, the pronunciation of as simple a word as *after* will not be generally the same in the southern part of the United States as in the eastern, and neither form will be heard commonly in the middle west.

Oftentimes even within a community, varying pronunciations may be heard. Despite these divergences there are certain standards that are accepted in the main for cultured and effective speech. In the first place, a pleasant quality of voice is a requisite. Secondly, dialect pronunciation and expressions are not permissible. For example, it would not be correct to say *lidy* (*i* as in *tidy*) for *lady*, *wit* or *wid* for *with*, *git* for *get*, even if the voice is well modulated and pleasing.

Furthermore, although a stilted and affected manner of speaking is considered poor form, it is not good English to run words together as *this'n* for *this one; gimme* for *give me; th'snoon* for *this noon; haryu* for *how are you; 'sneedless* for *it's needless.* Moreover, in standard and correct English, it is not good usage to substitute one sound for another as, *dooty* for *duty; singin'* for *singing; yu* for *you; hat* for *had; dontchu* for *don't you; latter* for *ladder; luf* for *love.* One should also avoid omitting sounds as in *kep'* for *kept; an'* for *and; 'em* for *them; 'bout* for *about; pome* for *poem.*

It would be difficult to give a definition of standard English that would be entirely satisfactory to everyone. Perhaps it will suffice to say that it is the careful choosing and enunciating of words. It has been described as "the speech which is least likely to attract attention to itself as being peculiar to any class or locality when heard by educated and cultured people."

You are probably saying, "What has all this to do with singing?" It is true that the statements about pronunciation and enunciation have referred specifically to speaking, nevertheless they apply with equal force to singing, for we carry our speech habits into song and vice versa. In both forms of vocal expression, vowel sounds should be pure and consonants should be clear-cut. Proper accent and stress of syllables, as well as right choice of sounds should be carefully considered.

At times, pronunciation of words in singing differs from that in speaking. This is especially true with regard to full pronunciation of vowels in unaccented syllables. In singing, the second syllables of such words as *patient*, *heaven*, *angel*, *maiden*, *emblem* should be pronounced with the sound *e* as in *pen* and not with *u* as in *cup*. The vowels in the final syllables of *wonderful*, *mindful*, *careful* are the same as in *look* or *put*. It may not be amiss to remind you that the definite article *the* is pronounced *thu* (*u* as in *up*) before words beginning with consonants, and *thi* [1] (*i* as in *it*) before vowels in both speaking and singing. The indefinite article *a* (as *a book; a song*) is an unstressed sound similar to the vowel in *up* or *of*.

## EXERCISES

1. Say the following distinctly and correctly:

> An ocean; a notion.
> A nice box; an ice box.
> This sage; this age.
> Take care; take air.
> Like clocks; like locks.
> Whither went the witch? Which witch?
> All's well that ends well.
> Sweetest sweets of summer's keeping.

The tip of the tongue should touch the upper teeth or teeth ridge for the sounds *n* and *t* in *don't;* it should be against the lower teeth before sounding *y* in *you*.

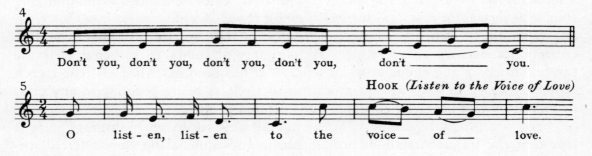

---

[1] Sometimes the sound of the definite article *the* before vowels is said to resemble *ee* as in *see*, but this comparison is not altogether accurate, for the sound heard in *the* is lax or weak, whereas that in *see* is stressed or strong.

# In the Time of Roses

Luise Reichardt
(1780–1826)

The composer of this song was a singer and a teacher of singing. Written by an obscure artist in a period when such composers as Beethoven, Mendelssohn, Schubert, and Schumann were giving the world a wealth of music, this song has nevertheless survived because of its sincerity and simplicity. That it is still sung and enjoyed today proves its merits. It should be sung with even phrasing and flexible rhythm. In the measures where triplet and quadruplet groupings of notes occur, there may be a slight rubato, but they should be sung evenly and accurately. Pure, legato tone and clear, distinct enunciation are necessary to bring out the meaning and beauty of words and music.

# Fiddle and I

ARTHUR GOODEVE

It is an interesting and valuable experience to sing with accompaniment other than the piano. An elementary, or simple, introduction is through the use of the *obbligato*, such as is furnished by the optional violin part for this song. Although not indispensable, it adds musical interest to the composition.

The song presents some problems in pronunciation, particularly in such combinations of sounds as *dl* (in *fiddle*), in the final syllables of such words as *river*, *ever*, *winter*, *together*, and in the vowel sounds in *fair* and *world*.

Creep - ing un - der barns so glad - ly When out-side the win - ter howls,

Play - ing sad - ly, play - ing mad - ly, Wak - ing up the rats and owls.

Ah! it was gay, night and day, Fair and cloud - y weath-er,

Fid-dle and I,   wan-der-ing by,   O-ver the world to - geth-er;

Fid-dle and I,   wan-der-ing by,   O-ver the world to - geth - er;

Down   by the wil - low,   Sum-mer-nights I

lie, _____ Flow'rs for my pil - low, And for roof the

sky; _____ Play - ing all my heart re-mem - bers, Old, old songs from

far a - way; Gold - en Junes and bleak De-cem - bers Rise a-round me

On, on for-ev-er, Till the jour-ney ends, Who shall dis-sev-er Us two trust-y friends

O-ver the world to-geth - er.

Who can bring the past be-fore me, Make the fu - ture gai - ly glow,

Lift the clouds that dark - en o'er me, Like my trust - y fid - dle

bow?_____ Ah! it was gay, night and day,

Fair and cloud-y weath-er, ___ Fid-dle and I, wan-der-ing by,

O-ver the world to-geth-er, ___ Fid-dle and I, wan-der-ing by,

O-ver the world to-geth ___ er.

# CLASS LESSONS IN SINGING

## QUESTIONS AND ACTIVITIES

1. Give examples of words which vary in pronunciation in different sections of the country or in your own vicinity.
2. What is meant by "standard English speech?"
3. Enumerate some of the errors in pronunciation commonly heard in ordinary conversation.
4. State reasons why careful pronunciation is important in both speaking and singing.
5. Give specific illustrations of words where pronunciation in singing differs from correct pronunciation in speaking.
6. Pronounce correctly the following words:

| blew | pretty | often | dance | dispute | pitiful | handsome | true | blue | mute |
| soft | emblem | water | while | grasped | torrent | interest | tune | due | rue |
| wash | gentle | poets | asked | whistle | capture | thankful | rule | June | lute |

7. Study exercises and songs in this lesson for words presenting common problems in pronunciation.
8. Look up the definition of "obbligato" and note what the word describes in present-day usage.

## SUPPLEMENTARY LIST OF MUSIC

Unison — Serenade — *Raff.* F(c-d), A♭(e♭-f)
S A — Boats of Mine — *Miller*
S S A — Little Boy Blue — *Nevin*
T T B B — Last Night — *Kjerulf*
S A T B — O Mary Don't You Weep — *Negro Spiritual*

**LOTTE LEHMANN**

Lyric soprano, opera and concert artist

*Courtesy George Maillard Kesslere, B. P.*

# 17

## ARTICULATION

*Speak the speech, I pray you as I pronounced it
to you trippingly on the tongue; but if you mouth it as
many of our players do, I had as lief the town crier
spake my lines.*

— Shakespeare

A song is a combination of words and melody. Devoid of either element it loses its identity. In truth, a purpose of singing is to interpret or translate words so as to strengthen ideas set forth in the text in an artistic way.

All too seldom does one find a vocalist who fulfills to a high degree this mission. It is not always a simple thing to do so, for the nature of the words, as well as the range and tempo of the music, sometimes makes it difficult to enunciate clearly. Nevertheless, the listener has the right, within limits, to expect an intelligible rendition of a song, and the singer should bend every effort to satisfy such expectation.

To articulate distinctly and fluently requires lingual and labial dexterity which, although not always inherent in a voice, can usually be acquired by practice.

### EXERCISES

Practice exercises slowly at first then as fast as clear, distinct articulation will permit.

1.

A big black bug bit a big black bear.

Eight great gray geese
Grazing gaily into Greece.

Some shun sunshine; do you shun sunshine?

Five wise wives weave withered withes.

A tooter who tooted the flute,
Tried to tutor two tutors to toot,
Said the two to the tooter,
"Is it easier to toot,
Than to tutor two tutors to toot?"

Peter Piper picked a peck of pickled peppers,
If Peter Piper picked a peck of pickled peppers,
How many peppers did Peter Piper pick?

How much wood could a woodchuck chuck,
If a woodchuck could chuck wood?
If a woodchuck could chuck all the wood he would chuck,
A woodchuck could chuck wood.

She says she sells seashells by the seashore,
And the shells she sells are seashells, I'm sure.

Peter Prangle, the prickly, prangly pear-picker
Picked three pecks of prickly, prangly pears
From the prangly pear trees on the pretty, pleasant prairies.

Theophilus Thistle, the successful thistle sifter,
In sifting a sieve full of unsifted thistles
Thrust three thousand thistles
Through the thick of his thumb.

Amidst the mists and coldest frosts,
With stoutest wrists and loudest boasts,
He thrusts his fists against the posts,
And still insists he sees the ghosts.

## QUESTIONS AND ACTIVITIES

1. Give reasons why it is sometimes difficult to articulate clearly and distinctly in singing.
2. Why is the practice of tongue twisters and songs with quick succession of words valuable in the study of singing?  How do they help in speech?
3. Formulate exercises other than those listed here that would be useful to you in acquiring dexterity in quick articulation.
4. Find phrases in songs previously studied that require quick articulatory changes.
5. What is a "madrigal"?
6. Report briefly on the English madrigalists.
7. Describe the means used by a concert artist you may have heard to convey mood, such as humor, pathos, to his audience.

## SUPPLEMENTARY LIST OF MUSIC

Unison — Pretty Polly Oliver — *Old English*.  C(a-d), E♭(c-f)
S A — Come Lasses and Lads — *Old English*
S S A — Follow Me Down to Carlow — *Fletcher*
T T B B — Tinkers' Chorus from "Robin Hood" — *DeKoven*
S A T B — Sir Eglamore — *Old English Song* arr. by *Gardiner*

# Long Ago in Alcala

F. W. WEATHERLY

ANDRÉ MESSAGER
(1853–1929)

André Messager was an eminent organist, conductor, and composer of light operas in the French style. Parisian critics have referred to his writing as "refined, melodious, and skillful, but often lacking in originality and force." Nevertheless, his works have gaiety, refinement, and musicianship quite unusual in the light opera field.

The song that appears here has vocal values for the student of singing, for it requires lingual and tonal dexterity to render it satisfactorily. Every word needs to be sung distinctly. The absurdity of the text is amusing for both singer and listener. Although inconsequential or trivial musically, the song is useful technically and as a concert encore which gives the singer an opportunity for characterization.

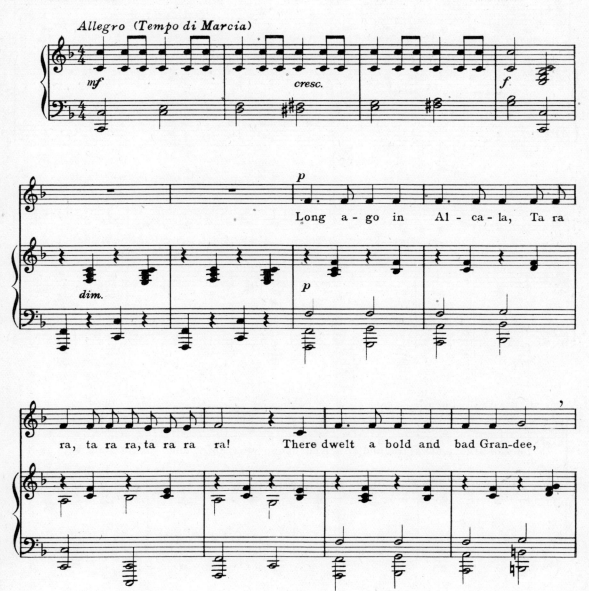

Who used to sail up-on the sea, to sail up-on the sea, to sail up-on the

sea, Ta ra ra, ta ra ra! He

lov'd a—maid of Al-ca-la, Ta ra ra, ta ra ra, ta ra ra ra! For

he was fine, and frank,and free, And she was fair as a maid could be, as a

maid could be! Tra la la, tra la la!

He was a ter-ri-ble, tall Al-ca-de, She was a love-ly

la-dy, Al-ca, Al-ca, Al-ca-de-da! The love-ly la-dy of Al-ca-la, the

la-dy of Al-ca-la! Ta ra ra, ta ra ra! They

met one eve in Al - ca - la, Ta ra ra, ta ra ra, ta ra ra

ra! He said, "Sweet maid - en, come with me," But

*parlando*

she was as coy as a maid should be, as a maid, as a

maid, as a maid should be! Tra la la, tra la

la! _____ So they said a - way, both he and she, Ta ra ra, ta ra ra, ta ra ra ra! Which was ra - ther odd, as it seems to me, For Al - ca - la _ is-n't on the sea, It's no - where near the sea! Tra la la la la la! Still,

that's the tale of the tall Al - ca - de, Who sail'd a - way with the love-ly la-dy, Al-

ca, Al - ca, Al - ca - de - da! Tra la la, tra la

la, tra la la la la! Now, if you know what this

song's a-bout, Ta ra ra, ta ra ra, ta ra ra ra! You know more than I do,

there's no doubt! It's a song we could ver-y well do with-out, we could ver-y well do with-out! Ta ra ra, ta ra ra! Yet to tell the_truth, it seems to me, Ta ra ra, ta ra ra, ta ra ra ra! Some songs are ver-y like this, you see, For from sen-si-ble words they are of-ten free, They are

bald,　　they are bald　　as a　　song　can　　be! Tra la la, tra la

la, tra la la　la la　la! _____

*p*

So when you sing such a　song as this, Ta ra　ra, ta ra ra, ta ra ra

*con sentimento*

ra!　　All a - bout a man, and a maid, and a kiss, And a　se-cret e - lope-ment and

wed - ded bliss (They're all— ver- y much like this) Tra la la la la

la. So long as the tune has a right good swing, It

does-nt much mat-ter what words you sing, Tra la la, Tra la la, tra la

la la la! Tra la la, tra la la, tra la la, tra la!

# Now is the Month of Maying

Thomas Morley
(1557–1603)

Thomas Morley was another of the gifted composers who brought luster to the reign of good Queen Bess. Many of his songs are still sung today, but probably none is better known and more popular than "Now is the Month of Maying." The "fa la la" refrain, characteristic of madrigals, is excellent for developing flexibility in the voice, and may well be used in various keys as a vocalise. The song should be sung rapidly and lightly, as indicated. The repeated phrases are effective when sung pianissimo.

Although intended to be sung in parts by several voices, the melody is interesting enough so that it may be used as a unison song, if desired. When sung in parts, it should be unaccompanied.

# 18

## DICTION

*So all my best is dressing old words new.*

— Shakespeare

Diction is the way or style of pronouncing words. It embraces the manner of utterance of component parts as vowels, consonants, and syllables, and the relation of one word to another.

Good diction in singing means correct pronunciation, distinct and quick articulation, and right tone production. It requires that the breath be sufficient and well controlled and that the articulatory organs be highly flexible. Although it is necessary for singers to modify vowel sounds to a certain extent in order to produce pleasing tones, yet they should learn to do so in such a manner that sound will impress the hearer clearly. It should be a definite aim of the singer to render songs so that the words can be understood and yet not disturb the perfect and even production of sound. To do so is a test of artistry and is what is meant by "good diction."

* Sometimes it is troublesome to pronounce some words in a song. For example, to sing a high note with a word which ends with a particular consonant may be difficult and to form it in the usual way may ruin the quality of tone. You can sometimes solve the problem if you sing the vowel and then practically speak the consonant. This requires that you stop the singing sound for a fraction of a second before you pronounce the consonant. To illustrate, if you have the word "boat" to sing on high *a*, sing *boa* then quietly say the *t*.

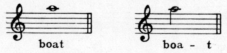

Whereas it sometimes may be hard to produce a final consonant and still maintain right tonal quality, a consonant at the beginning of a word on a high tone usually helps place the tone. Pronounce it thoughtfully and place the consonant on the same level as the vowel.

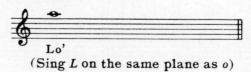

# DICTION

An easily produced voice can help clumsy diction; good diction can improve voice placing.[1] It is an interchangeable system. Sometimes by placing a tone a little more carefully, you find that a syllable which seemed difficult to pronounce can be handled more comfortably. Then again when a tone, usually a high one or a low one, seems hard to place, by pronouncing your syllable skillfully, the tone suddenly is placed. *E. L.*

## QUESTIONS AND ACTIVITIES

1. Define the word "diction."
2. What is meant by the term "good diction" in speaking and singing?
3. Read aloud the words to the songs given in this lesson. Compare your reading with others in the class. Whose diction was most artistic? Why?
4. Sing the songs and make the same comparison.

## SUPPLEMENTARY LIST OF MUSIC

Unison — I Know a Hill — *Whelpley*. C♯ mi (c♯–c♯), F♯ mi (f♯–f♯)
S A — In Summer Woods — *Ireland*
S S A — Night Song — *Clokey*
T T B B — Annie Laurie — *Scotch Song*
S A T B — O Hush Thee, My Babie — *Sullivan*

---

[1] The term "voice placing" is used frequently by teachers of singing. "To place the voice" means to shape the oral cavity and control the breath in such manner that there is proper use of the vocal modifiers and resonators. Specifically, good placement means that tones are produced easily and effectively.

# Who is Sylvia?

Franz Schubert
(1797–1828)

The verses, "Who is Sylvia," are found in Act IV, scene ii, of the play, "Two Gentlemen of Verona," by Shakespeare. They were written by Thurio, one of Sylvia's lovers, to extol her charms and were sung by him and a group of hired musicians in the hope that he (Thurio) might win her favor.

The song is in strophic form. To bring out the beauty of the melody and words, it should be sung with proper tone color and careful diction. As with all Schubert's songs, the accompaniment merits attention and study, for it contributes greatly to the proper interpretation.

heav'ns such grace did lend____ her,
help him of his blind - ness;
on the dull earth dwell - ing;

And

That ad - mir - ed she might____
be - ing help'd____ in - hab - its
To her____ gar - lands let us____

be,____
there,____ And be - ing help'd in - hab - its____
bring,____ To her gar - lands let us____

That ad - mir - ed she might

be.
there.
bring.

# The Sailor's Life

H. Lane Wilson, the English baritone, composer, and arranger of folk songs, is best known in America for his waltz song, "Carmena." "The Sailor's Life"[1] appears in his unusual collection of "Old English Songs." It is a typical example of the sea songs so characteristic of music in England. Its style suggests that it was written by some composer long forgotten or entirely unknown. Although probably not a folk song in the true sense of the term, its melodic and structural simplicity gives it the folk flavor.

It should be sung in a fairly rapid tempo, with rollicking joviality. Study the words carefully for correct pronunciation and accent. Sing the second syllables of such words as *little*, *fiddle*, *danger*, and *cheerly* with less stress than the first syllables. Use the refrain as a vocalize for achieving rapid and clean-cut diction.

[1] From "OLD ENGLISH MELODIES" by H. Lane Wilson (complete Collection, $2.00) published by Boosey & Company, New York, U.S.A.

per-ils ga-ther round, All sense of dan-ger's drowned, We des-
per-ils ga-ther round, All sense of dan-ger's drowned, We des-

*a tempo*

pise it to— a man; } We sing a lit-tle, and laugh a lit-tle, And
pise it to— a man; }

*colla voce*

*a tempo*

work a lit-tle, and play a lit-tle, And fid-dle a lit-tle, and

foot it a lit-tle, As brave-ly as— we can. We

*can.*

*Dal Segno*
*Verse 2 %*

3. But think not that our life is hard, Though

storms at sea ill - treat us; For com - ing home's a

sweet re - ward, When wives and sweet - hearts greet us, When

*colla voce*

perils gather round All sense of danger's drowned, We des-
pise it to a man; We sing a little, and laugh a little, And
work a little, and play a little, And fiddle a little, and
foot it a little, As brave-ly as we can, We

sing a lit-tle, and laugh a lit-tle, And work a lit-tle, and

play a lit-tle, And fid-dle a lit-tle, and foot it a lit-tle, As

brave-ly as — we can, As brave-ly as — we can, As

brave-ly as we can.

# 19

## INTONATION AND ATTACK OF TONE

*How will you know the pitch of that great bell,*
*Too large for you to stir?  Let but a flute*
*Play neath the fine-mixed metal!  Listen close*
*Till the right note flows forth a silvery rill.*

— Eliot

Intonation is the manner of playing or singing a tone in regard to pitch. Singing off pitch, or "out of tune," is heard all too frequently and is one of the glaring faults found among singers.  It may be due to failure to hear the tone exactly or correctly.  It is often caused by incorrect breathing and improper use of the resonating cavities (faulty voice placing), tense throat and articulatory organs, poor formation of words, forcing the voice, or repressing the voice.  If you are tired or are not feeling well, you may sing off pitch.  Nervousness in singing before people likewise may contribute to faulty intonation.

At times if you become disinterested in what you are singing or are careless or inattentive, your voice may flat in pitch.  On the other hand, it may happen that you put forth too great an effort in your zeal to do well and cause your voice to sharp in pitch.

Poorly ventilated rooms or trying climatic conditions frequently induce incorrect intonation.  An inappropriate selection of music also may bring about this defect.  For example, the range of the composition may not be suited to your voice, the phrases may be too long, or the intervals too difficult.  Possibly you may not know the music well enough to be certain of the pitches.

In rare instances, imperfect hearing or tone deafness is the origin of the difficulty.  Unfortunately in such cases there is little that can be done to help those so afflicted, and such persons must face the fact that they can never become singers.

If you have a tendency to sing off pitch, find the cause, for it suggests the cure.  Generally if the pitch is flat, exercises sung with the sounds *hm*, *hn*, *nay*, *nee*, *my*, *see-ah* are helpful.  If you sing sharp, try such combinations as *soh*, *faw*, *lah*, and so forth.  * Place your voice carefully, pronounce your words correctly, try to co-ordinate the position of your voice with the position of your words, — have them on the same plane, — then support your tone properly (breathe and use breath correctly), and you will usually sing in tune.  That is, unless you have a bad ear, and then you should not sing at all!  *E. L.*

As a rule, if one has a good ear, a normal vocal organ, and fair musical sense, intonation need not be defective. It is important that you train yourself to listen to pitch of tone in your own and other voices and in instruments. Thereby you will cultivate a critical ear. Practice reproducing pitches without instrumental aid, but, until you have developed a good feeling for pitch, it is well to check yourself frequently with an accurately tuned piano or pitch pipe.

In connection with intonation it should be pointed out that the way you begin a tone is extremely important. You cannot start it with incorrect intonation, poor tonal quality, and indistinct articulation and be able entirely to rectify your mistakes. Indeed, you must know what you wish to produce and how to do it before you commence singing. Famous Italian teachers of the past called the starting of a tone *attacare*, meaning "to attack." They considered it highly important and insisted upon their pupils doing it satisfactorily.

The finish of tones should also receive careful attention. As they begin, so should they end, — exactly in tune and well controlled.

EXERCISES

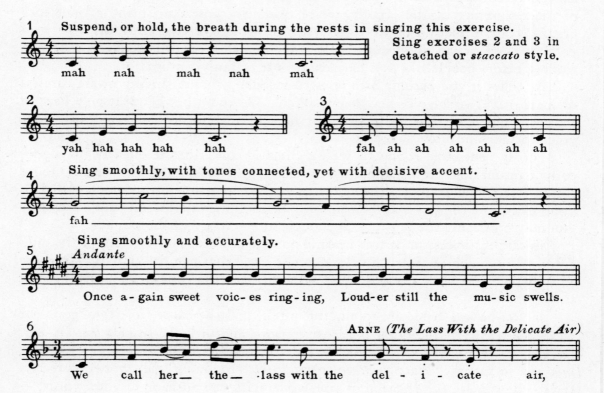

# The Monotone

PETER CORNELIUS
(1824-1874)

Cornelius first took up the profession of an actor but soon abandoned it for a musical and literary career in which he achieved considerable success. The song "The Monotone" is one of the most familiar and interesting of his compositions. It gives expression to a man's thoughts concerning his sweetheart who has died. The song should be sung in a contemplative manner, with a variety of tone color to express different emotions contained in each sentence. The melodic interest of the song lies in the accompaniment, for the voice part is written entirely on one tone. To attack the same note again and again with accuracy of intonation and in correct time requires vocal and musical ability of no small order. For this reason this song may well be transposed into other keys and sung with various vowel and consonant sounds (as *noh, fah, mah,* etc.), as well as the words, thus giving added opportunity to acquire vocal skill in the attack and release of tone.

This is the first song for which the text has also been provided in the original foreign language. The correct pronunciation of German offers its own problems. If you are not familiar with the language, your teacher will coach you. If you are planning to take up singing as a vocation, you will need to know German because German "lieder" are the foundation of an artist's repertoire.[1]

---

[1] General rules for the pronunciation of German, French, and Italian are given beginning on page 195.

Ah, can it be the last faint breath That stirr'd thy
*Ist es der Hauch, der dir ent - schwebt, als ein - mal*

pal-lid lips ere death? Is it the
*noch dein Mund ge - bebt?* *Ist es des*

ten-der mon - o - tone Of church-bell which for thee made moan?
*Glöck-leins trü - ber Klang, der dir ge - folgt den Weg ent - lang?*

Lo, still it comes so full, so clear, As though thy
*Mir klingt der Ton so voll, so rein, als schlöss er*

soul were float - ing    near,  
*dei - ne  See - le    ein,*  

As though with  love    and yearn-ing deep  You sang my  bit-ter pain    to  
*als  stie - gest  lie - bend nie - der  Du    und  sän-gest  mei-nen Schmerz  in*  

sleep!  
*Ruh!*

# The Postillion

F. W. WEATHERLY

JAMES LYMAN MOLLOY
(1837-1909)

James Lyman Molloy, an Irish musician, composed and arranged many popular songs. Among his best known works are "Love's Old Sweet Song" and "The Kerry Dance."

The "postillion" is a post rider or a fore-runner for a post. In former times he rode one of the horses drawing a coach or chaise, to act as a guide. Bristol, referred to in the song, is a town situated on the Avon River in West England.

This song should be sung with definite accent and with flowing rhythm. The tempo should be fairly fast and should be kept generally exact, except where markings indicate that a slower rate of speed is desirable for interpretative and vocal effects.

1. The night is late, we dare not wait, the winds be-gin to
2. Oh, I've a wife in Bris-tol town, a wife and chil-dren

blow, —— An' 'ere we gain the hol-low plain, there'll be a storm, I
three, —— An' they are sleep-ing safe and sound, But she keeps watch for

trow; —— An' as —— we pass the Beg-gar's tree, look out'n the dark, look
me; —— An' who would quake the road —— to take with such a prize in

out, \_\_\_\_ The phan-tom horse-man   you will see, He'll\_ crack his whip and
store,\_\_\_ Though rav-ens croak on   Hang-man's oak, And a storm be at   our

shout: \_ Ho - lâ!   Ho-lâ!   Ho - lâ! \_\_\_ He'll\_ crack his whip and
fore: \_ Ho - lâ!   Ho-lâ!   Ho - lâ! \_\_\_ And a storm be at   our

shout, Ho - lâ!   Ho - lâ!   Ho - lâ! _____ Who's for the coach to -
fore, Ho - lâ!   Ho - lâ!   Ho - lâ! _____ Who's for the coach to -

night, \_\_\_ For   we   are boun' for   Bris-tol town be - fore\_ the morn-ing
night, \_\_\_ For   we   are boun' for   Bris-tol town be - fore\_ the morn-ing

**Poco più lento**

3. Then one glass more, the ale is fine, A toast, sweet la - dies fair,— To

each man's home, good mas - ters mine, and may— he soon be there.— The

*ritard*     *poco rall.*
*colla voce*     *poco rall*

**a tempo**

sparks shall flash as on— we dash, The clatt'-ring wheels shall spin,— And

ev - 'ry sleep - ing loon shall stir, To see the coach roll in:— Ho -

là! Ho-là! Ho - là!____ To see the coach roll in; Ho -

_(gaily)_

là! Ho-là! Ho - là!____ Who's for the coach to - night,____ For

_riten._

we are boun' for Bris - tol town, Be - fore__ the morn - ing light. Ho -

_rall._

là!____ Ho - là! Ho-là! Ho - là!____

_colla voce_

Ped.

# INTONATION AND ATTACK OF TONE

## QUESTIONS AND ACTIVITIES

1. What is meant by "intonation?"
2. Indicate some of the common causes of poor intonation.
3. Suggest ways in which one may overcome such faults.
4. Define the Italian word "attacare."
5. Discuss and illustrate the correct way of beginning and ending tones.
6. Take a suitable pitch from a well-tuned instrument, then sing the ascending and descending major scale without accompaniment. Check yourself with the original pitch when you have finished singing. Was your intonation accurate or inaccurate?
7. Sing a song without instrumental aid. Is your pitch correct throughout the composition?
8. Practice singing different intervals both up and down from a given pitch as, for example, major second, major third, minor third, perfect fourth, perfect fifth, augmented fifth, major sixth, etc. Test your pitch with an instrument after you have sung the second tone.
9. Think, then sing a pitch in the medium part of your voice, as, for example, A'. After singing it check yourself with an instrument. Did you recall and reproduce the pitch correctly?

## SUPPLEMENTARY LIST OF MUSIC

Unison —   Hark, Hark the Lark — *Schubert*.  B♭ (f–f), A♭ (e♭–e♭)
S A —        Amaryllis — *Ghys-Ambrose*
S S A —    Lift Thine Eyes — *Mendelssohn*
T T B B — High Barbary — *Traditional Chantey* arr. by *Hall*
S A T B — The Holly and the Ivy — *Traditional Carol* arr. by *Thiman*

MARIA JERITZA

Lyric soprano, as Nedda in Leoncavallo's *I Pagliacci*

# 20

## LEGATO AND SOSTENUTO

*What joys to capture song from sound*
*And send it throbbing through the hearts of men.*

— Selinger

The words *legato* and *sostenuto* mean, respectively, *to connect* and *to sustain*. Whether a song is fast or slow, sad or gay, simple or difficult, it is necessary for its successful rendition to go from one tone to the next smoothly and with accurate intonation. To do this the voice must be freely produced and the breath ample to sustain the tone and carry the phrase to the end.

Closely associated with *legato* style is *portamento*, or carrying the voice from one pitch to another with a delicate glide. It is distinguished from *legato* by the fact that pitches between the limiting tones are lightly sounded. The *portamento* must be done lightly, smoothly, and exactly, with no suggestion of force. It should be employed only at appropriate places in the composition and should never even faintly suggest what is commonly known as "scooping" often heard in untrained and inartistic singing. If the composer wishes this effect, he usually indicates it by using a slur, or curved line, or the phrase "portando la voce" (carrying the voice).

The opposite of *legato* and *sostenuto* singing is *staccato*[1] or detached style of vocalization, where each tone is attacked, then released quickly so that definite intervals of silence occur between them.

Smooth, flowing delivery of voice, or *legato* singing, was the foundation of the Italian *bel canto* art of the seventeenth century. It is as important in the equipment of the singer today, for upon it depend all vocal graces.

### EXERCISES

Sing the following exercises slowly and smoothly.

118

[1] See exercises nos. 2, 3, and 6, page 108, and exercise no. 7, page 125.

# LEGATO AND SOSTENUTO

OLD ENGLISH AIR (*Drink to Me Only With Thine Eyes*)

Drink to me on-ly with thine eyes, and I will pledge with mine.

*Larghetto*

SCHUMANN (*The Lotus Flower*)

The Lo-tus flow'r doth lan-guish Un-der the sun's warm light.

## QUESTIONS AND ACTIVITIES

1. Define the Italian words *legato* and *sostenuto* as they pertain to singing.
2. What style of singing is closely associated with *legato*? Discuss this manner, or way of rendition, pointing out common faults in its performance.
3. What is the opposite of *legato* style called? Explain what the term means.
4. Demonstrate the different styles of singing mentioned above.
5. Give reasons why the songs "Dedication" by Franz and "Thou'rt Lovely as a Flower" by Schumann are presented in this lesson.
6. Tell briefly of Schumann's life and his contribution to music as composer, piano virtuoso, and critic.
7. Compare Robert Franz' work as a song writer with Schubert's and Schumann's.

## SUPPLEMENTARY LIST OF MUSIC

Unison — Marie — *Franz.* D (b–d), F (d–f)
S A — Prayer from "Haensel and Gretel" — *Humperdinck*
S S A — Slumber Song — *Gretchaninoff*
T T B B — Drink to Me Only With Thine Eyes — *Old English*
S A T B — Beautiful Savior — arr. by *Christiansen*

# Dedication

WOLFGANG MÜLLER

ROBERT FRANZ
(1815–1892)

Robert Franz, one of the greatest lyric writers in the history of music, was a man of broad musicianship and culture. Like Schubert, his genius was, to a great extent, unrecognized by his compatriots during his lifetime. In his later years, he became deaf and thus handicapped was saved from dire need only by the help of friends.

For the theme of his songs, Franz usually selected love and the beauties of Nature. These he composed in an intimate manner in simple strophic form. In them, melody, accompaniment, and words are closely linked. He strove at all times to express the meaning of the words and succeeded admirably in doing so.

The song "Dedication" is typical of many of his compositions. It undoubtedly is one of the best known and most popular. Here the student will find opportunity for the employment of legato, or sustained, tone.

Thine have they ev - er been, thine on - ly. So clear in thy
*Dein sind sie al - le ja ge - we - sen. Aus Dei - ner*

love - ly eyes, they shone, Ra - diant in beau - ty I did but
*lie - ben Au - gen Licht hab' ich sie treu - lich ab - ge -*

read them; Dost thou not know they are thine own?
*le - sen, kennst Du die eig - nen Lie - der nicht?*

Dost thou not know they are thine own?
*kennst Du die eig - nen Lie - der nicht?*

# Thou'rt Lovely as a Flower

HEINRICH HEINE
Translated by NATALIE McFARREN

ROBERT SCHUMANN
(1810–1856)

Although Schubert is usually thought of whenever songs of the Romantic Period are mentioned, Schumann's contributions are equally matchless for their flawless beauty. Not only was this composer a great musician, but he was also an able writer and critic in the field of music. His broad education, poetic insight, romantic imagination, and rare musical genius, with his fearless, independent, and sincere nature have combined to give him a unique place in the history of music.

The poem "Du Bist Wie Eine Blume," by Heinrich Heine, has had many musical settings, but none is more perfectly wedded to the text or more genuine in its sentiment than this one by Schumann. To sing it satisfactorily, the voice should be well sustained and mellow in tone, expressing a quiet, happy, reflective mood. The phrasing should be broad in effect without dragging.

A musician's educational background is not complete unless he is familiar with much of Schumann's music, such as the Concerto in A-minor for piano and orchestra, the string quartet and quintet with piano, and the songs "Two Grenadiers," "The Lotus Flower," and "Dedication."

Steals o'er my heart's de-light, I long_____ on those gold-en
*schleicht mir in's Herz hin-ein.* *Mir ist,_____ als ob ich die*

tress-es My fold-ed hands__ to lay,
*Hän-de auf's Haupt dir le - gen sollt',*

Pray-ing that Heav'n may pre-serve thee So fair, so pure al-
*be - tend, dass Gott dich er-hal - te so rein und schön und*

way.
*hold.*

# 21

## FLEXIBILITY

*I pray thee,*
*I pray thee,*
   *How do we best sing a scale?*
*Tra-la-la-la-la-la-la-la*
*Tra-la-la-la-la-la-la-la,*
   *This is the way*
   *To sing a scale.*

\* In order that your voice may respond quickly to change of pitch and words, it must have considerable flexibility. The development of a technique which permits you to make vocal adjustments rapidly and precisely gives lightness to tone which is desirable and necessary either in singing a slow, sustained song or a fast, staccato one.

Perhaps your voice may not have natural flexibility. Nevertheless, you should strive to acquire it as much as possible. Practice scales and arpeggios slowly at first, gradually increasing the tempo as you gain skill. Whatever the rate of speed, the tone should always be smooth and easily produced, the pitch exact and true, and the time and rhythm correct and flowing.

### EXERCISES

\*In practicing scales, the following suggestions or hints may prove helpful: In a five note scale, the tone that often causes trouble or "sticks" is the third one. Accent it. Once you have passed the third tone, the scale moves along smoothly and easily, as a rule. In a nine note scale, accent the fifth tone. If it still "sticks," begin the scale with *see* and change to *ah* on the fifth note. *EL.*

5 see ___ ah _____

13 SWEDISH FOLK SONG (*When I was Seventeen*)

la    la ___ la    la    la ___ la    la    la ___ la    la

la    la    la    la ___ la    la    la ___ la    la    la    la    la ___ la

14 *Molto cresc.*    PURCELL (*Nymphs and Shepherds*)

Whilst you ex - press _____ your jol - li - try.

# I Attempt from Love's Sickness to Fly

Sir Robert Howard

Henry Purcell
(1658–1695)

Henry Purcell is acclaimed by many as the greatest English composer of all time. Certain it is that he excelled musicians of the period in which he lived in every form in which he wrote. In referring to *Dido and Aeneas*, Holst says: "Purcell wrote the only perfect English opera ever written," and Playford declares that "he had a peculiar genius to express the energy of English words."

Purcell is said to have been the first English composer to use Italian musical terms to designate how he wished his music performed. He was also one of the first composers to write music for two violins, viola, and violoncello, — our modern string quartet.

The aria selected for this lesson is from the incidental music to the "Indian Queen," composed in 1693. The many diatonic or scale progressions, where one vowel sound is sung to several pitches, make it a valuable study to develop vocal agility. The first section of the composition therefore may be transposed into keys that do not carry the voice out of a comfortable range and used as a tonal drill with words as they appear in the song and with different vowels and with syllables, such as *fah; noh, moh;* etc.

fe-ver, Since I am my-self, my own fe-ver_ and pain. No

more now, no more now, fond_ heart, with pride should we swell, Thou

canst not_ raise forc-es, thou canst not_ raise forc-es e-nough to re-

bel, I at-tempt from Love's sick-ness to fly_____ in_

vain, Since I am my-self, my own fe-ver, Since I am my-

self, my own fe- ver_ and pain.

For love has more

pow'r and less mer - cy than fate, To make us_ seek ru - in, To_

make us— seek  ru - in, and  love  those that hate. I  at-tempt from Love's

sick-ness to fly_____ in— vain, Since  I  am  my-

self, my  own  fe-ver, Since  I  am  my-self, my  own  fe - ver— and—

pain.—

# Trip, Trip

Old English Country Dance

THEO. MARZIALS

The composer of this country dance was a Belgian baritone and the composer of many popular songs. His appointment in 1870 to the music section of the British Museum was evidence that he was a capable musician and familiar with musical literature.

The duet given here is a good example of canonic writing, a method of composition especially popular in the 16th and 17th centuries. In this form, a melody is imitated tone by tone or interval by interval by a second voice, or by three or more voices.

1st verse HE. Come and trip it on the fal-low, pret-ty maid, sweet maid, Come and
2nd verse SHE. If I trip it on the fal-low, pret-ty sir, sweet sir, If I

trip, trip, trip in the mer-ry, mer-ry shade, _____
trip, trip, trip, oh, my moth-er will de-mur, _____

For the fid-dlers are a fidd-ling and the bag-pipes play, And 'tis
Tho' the fid-dlers are a fidd-ling and the bag-pipes play, And 'tis

Spring, sweet maid, and ho - li - day.
Spring, sweet sir, and ho - li - day.

Come and sing, oh, sing in the

mer - ry, mer - ry Spring, When the sweet flow - ers blow and the

*1st verse* SHE.
*2nd verse* HE. Come and sing, oh, sing in the

young birds sing. Come and sing, oh, sing in the

me - ry, mer - ry Spring, When the sweet flow - ers blow and the

me - ry, mer - ry Spring, When the sweet flow-ers blow and the

young birds sing. Come and sing, oh, sing in the

young birds sing.

mer - ry, mer - ry Spring, When the sweet flow-ers blow and the young birds sing.

HE *mf*

Nay'tis meet and ve-ry pret-ty, pret-ty May, sweet May, Oh, to

SHE

If'tis meet and ve-ry pre-ty, pret-ty sir, sweet

15 Allegro — HANDEL (*from* Messiah)

We have turn - - - - - - ed

16 — HANDEL (*O Had I Jubal's Lyre*)

in songs like hers re - joi - - - ce, in songs like hers re-joice.

## QUESTIONS AND ACTIVITIES

1. Why is flexibility an important characteristic or quality in a voice?
2. Can flexibility of voice be developed or acquired? If so, how?
3. Why is the adage "make haste slowly" applicable to the singing of scales?
4. Devise at least three exercises similar to those given in this lesson.
5. Find passages or phrases in songs you have studied that have scale and arpeggio passages.
6. Define the word *canon* in music and tell something about the history of this form of writing.
7. Trace the development of vocal and instrumental music in Tudor England.
8. Give a short report on the life of Henry Purcell.

## SUPPLEMENTARY LIST OF MUSIC

Unison — Phyllis Has Such Charming Graces — *Old English* arr. by *Wilson*.
    Bb mi (db-gb), G mi (bb-eb)
S A — Come and Trip It — *Carmichael*
S S A — Where the Bee Sucks — *Dr. Arne-Bantock*
T T B B — When Love is Kind — *Old English*
S A T B — In These Delightful Pleasant Groves — *Purcell*

# 22

## MODES IN MUSIC

*. . . each tone of our scale in itself is naught:*
*It is everywhere in the world — loud, soft, and all is said:*
*Give it to me to use! I mix it with two in my thought:*
*And there! Ye have heard and seen: Consider and bow the head!*

— Browning

A scale, from the Latin word *scala* meaning "a ladder," is a series of tones arranged according to a certain prescribed plan or order. The evolution of their mode, or arrangement, as we know them today, extends over many centuries and provides an interesting and important development in the history of music.

Scales have changed, not only from time to time, but from place to place. Ancient Arabians divided their scale into seventeen tones; Chinese used, among others, a five-tone or pentatonic scale; and Hindus utilized as many as twenty-two tones. The ancient Greeks employed eight modes. Our modern scales, which we inherited from the Greeks, consist of eight tones. In addition, we have one constructed within the octave (eight-tone scale) which has twelve tones and is known as the chromatic scale. In modern terminology it is often referred to as the duodecuple scale. Some composers also use a scale of six tones, or a whole-tone scale.[1]

Much of the music we hear, however, is based on the eight-tone scales that have been in use since about the seventeenth century when the tempered scale came into practice. These are called the major and minor modes and are constructed on patterns of successive intervals one-whole step or one-half step apart. It is the difference in the sequence of the intervals that makes their individuality. The major scale conforms to one set pattern, but the minor has three forms, — natural, melodic, and harmonic.

With some composers a song is either major or minor. With others there is an intermingling of the two. For example, Schubert and Franz used first one and then the other at will to express the mood of the composition. Sir George Grove said: "With Schubert the minor mode seems to be synonymous with trouble and the major with relief; and the mere mention of the sun or a smile or any other emblem of gladness is sure to make him modulate."[2]

---

[1] See "Loch Lomond," page 70, for an example of a melody built on the six-tone scale.
[2] Finck, Henry T., *Songs and Song Writers* (Charles Scribner's Sons, N.Y., 1923), page 101.

Yet one should not assume that the major mode always expresses gladness and the minor mode sorrow. In fact, the reverse is sometimes true. However, as a rule, the minor mode is used by composers to express sorrow and mystery, and the major is used to portray joy and brightness.

## EXERCISES

Practice these exercises with different vowel and consonant combinations as suggested in previous lessons.

# Courage

Franz Schubert
(1797–1828)

This song is one that appears in the "Winter Journey" (Winterreise), a cycle of twenty-four songs. It describes the journey of a young lover and depicts in tone the various emotions of joy and depression experienced by him. Wilhelm Müller, a close friend of Schubert, wrote the poem. He also wrote the words of the cycle "The Beautiful Maid of the Mill" (Die schöne Müllerin).

The song "Courage" is a last manifestation of cheerfulness on the part of the despairing suitor. It is a good example of Schubert's tendency to shift quickly from one mode to another in accordance with the changing mood of the words. The English translation is used by permission of Alexander Dean from his adaptation of Schubert's opera "Rosamunde"[1] in which "Courage" has been interpolated.

The best known of the songs in "Winter Journey" is "The Linden Tree" (Der Lindenbaum) which has become so popular that many consider it a folk song.

When the snow___ flies in my face, Off I gai-ly___ brush it.
I heed not ___ what-e'er it says Ev-'ry cry dis - dain-ing,

When my ___ heart_____ 'plains in my
I'll not ___ hear_____ its bit - ter

---

[1] Rosamunde, a pastoral operetta in two acts, music by Franz Schubert, book by Alexander Dean, published by Silver Burdett Company, New York.

breast,    Loud I sing_to— hush it.
plea,    Fools are e'er com - plain - ing.

Joy - ous-ly we— face the world,    Fac - ing— wind_and— weath - er!

If there be no— gods on earth, We'll be gods to -

geth - er!    Joy - ous-ly we— face the world,

Fac - ing wind and— weath - er!    If there be no—

gods on earth, We'll be— gods to - geth - er!

# Out of My Deepest Sadness

Heinrich Heine
Translated by Seymour Barnard [1]

Robert Franz
(1815–1892)

Franz, as did also Schubert and Schumann, found in Heine's poems the inspiration for many of his songs. This short poem of eight lines is treated in a restrained, simple, and sincere way, well suited to the words. In keeping with their mood, Franz modulated freely from one mode to another.

The singer should render the song in an unaffected, straightforward way, with no irregularity of rhythm. The tone should be smooth and flowing. The accompaniment supports or follows the melody, thereby requiring perfect ensemble between singer and accompanist.

Out of my deep-est sad - ness
*Aus mei-nen gro-ssen Schmer - zen*

Ten-der-est songs are wak - ing. They soar far a-way in their
*mach ich die klei-nen Lie - der, die he-ben ihr kling-end Ge-*

glad - ness, Their flight to her heart — they're tak - - -
*fie - der und flat-tern nach ih - rem Her - - -*

[1] From *The Progressive Music Series*, Book Four, copyright, 1920, by permission of the publishers, Silver Burdett Company, New York.

ing.
zen.
So glad - ly I watch them wing - ing, And
*Sie fan - den den Weg zur Trau - ten, doch*

glad - ly I see them re - turn - ing; Re - turn - ing but ne'er in their
*kom - men sie wie - der und kla - gen, und kla - gen, und wol - len nicht*

sing - ing They whis - per the sto - ry they're learn - - -
*sa - gen, was sie im Her - zen schau - - -*

ing.
*ten.*

# CLASS LESSONS IN SINGING

## QUESTIONS AND ACTIVITIES

1. What is meant by the word *mode* in music?
2. Discuss musical scales of different peoples.
3. Make a brief report on the Greek modes.
4. What is the "tempered" scale and what developments led to its introduction?
5. Name forms of scales commonly used in our music today. From what people were they derived?
6. Point out differences in patterns in modern scales.
7. Analyze songs you have sung in previous lessons for different modes.
8. In the songs given in this lesson, where do modulations or changes of mode occur? Why do you think the composers made changes at these points? How did they effect, or bring about, modulation?
9. Read the Grove's Dictionary references how Sir Arthur Sullivan found the incomplete manuscript of Schubert's "Rosamunde" in an old house in Vienna a long time after the composer's death. (For complete reconstruction of the opera, see the complete edition published by Silver Burdett Company.)

## SUPPLEMENTARY LIST OF MUSIC

Unison — The Asra — *Rubinstein.* G mi (d-ab), E mi (b-f)
S A — In His Little Cradle — *Franck*
S S A — Legend — *Tschaikowsky*
T T B B — One Who Has Yearned Alone — *Tschaikowsky*
S A T B — Serenade — *Schubert*

CHARLES KULLMAN

Lyric tenor, concert and opera artist

# 23

## PHRASING

*Hark!  the numbers soft and clear*
*Gently steal upon the ear;*
*Now louder and yet louder rise,*
*And fill with spreading sound the skies.*

— Pope

A phrase in song may be defined as a unit of musical and verbal thought. As a rule, the composer sees that they coincide.  As in sentences, phrases in music vary in length, — some are short, others are long.  If a phrase in a song is broken in the wrong place, its musical and verbal continuity and meaning are sacrificed.  It is necessary, therefore, to study songs and exercises carefully in order to discover the correct phrasing.  Meaning and punctuation of sentences, breath marks, phrase lines, and cadences help you determine this.

In beginning the study of singing, vocalists often are unable to carry over a long series of tones easily and effectively.  As a consequence, the phrase has to be divided into smaller parts.  This should be done quickly and unobtrusively and only at proper points.  If training is correct, the number of tones a singer can produce in one breath should increase day by day.

To perform a long phrase satisfactorily is one of the most important factors in musical performance.  As has been indicated, this is a matter of vocal development to a great extent.  It is also a matter of courage.  If you do not have the mind or the will to sustain a number of tones in succession without breaking them, an adequate supply of breath and a pleasing voice avail little.

Although the direction "to phrase" often means "to breathe," the term *good phrasing* has considerably greater significance than the mere indication that breath has been replenished skillfully.  To phrase a song well denotes not only that you have taken breath correctly, but that you have built up climaxes properly and have rendered dynamic and other tonal effects intelligently and beautifully.  Indeed, good phrasing implies right use of voice in all respects.

### EXERCISES

Sing each of the following exercises and excerpts of songs on one breath.

(Exercises are continued on page 152.)

# Where E'er You Walk

GEORGE FREDERICK HANDEL
(1685–1759)

Handel, a native of Germany, spent most of his life in England. He came to be known as the outstanding English composer of his time. In fact, the vogue for his music long overshadowed Purcell, and it is only in recent years that the earlier composer has been fully appreciated in a truer perspective.

"The Messiah," the oratorio which Handel composed in twenty-four days for a charity concert, is probably the best known of his compositions. Unquestionably it is one of the greatest works in this form. Like Bach, Handel was famous as an organist as well as composer. By sad coincidence both men became blind in their later years.

Although Handel's operas are seldom given stage performances, many contain beautiful numbers that have remained as concert favorites. One of the most familiar is the aria for tenor from "Semele." In its slow, broad, dignified style it is characteristic of much of Handel's music. It should be sung in even tempo with smooth phrasing and legato tone, and with a real appreciation and feeling for the *bel canto* style of singing.

to— a shade.

Wher - e'er you tread, the blush-ing flow'rs shall rise, And

all things flou-rish, and all things flou-rish, Wher-

e'er you turn your eyes, Wher-e'er you turn your eyes, wher-e'er you turn your eyes.

D.C. al Fine

# Florian's Song

J. P. Claris de Florian
Translated by M. Louise Baum [1]

Benjamin Godard
(1849–1895)

Godard, a talented French composer, was first interested in becoming a violin virtuoso, but later he turned to composition. Although he does not rank with men of the greatest genius in the creative field, nevertheless he had considerable originality and a fine instinct for orchestral color. His compositions are numerous and of various types. Among them are several operas, symphonies, suites, concertos, chamber works, many piano pieces, and over one hundred songs. Probably the best known of his songs are the "Berceuse" from the opera "Jocelyn" and the "Florian's Song."

The song of "Florian" should be sung at a moderately quick tempo, with flowing, flexible rhythm, and with a good understanding and treatment of important and unimportant words and syllables. Care should be taken to phrase the song gracefully and correctly. Unless the phrases are well shaped and the climaxes properly prepared and rendered, the song tends to be jerky.

Students of harmony will find the accompaniment offers an interesting study in chord structure and sequence, and in the use of pedal-point in the first nine measures.

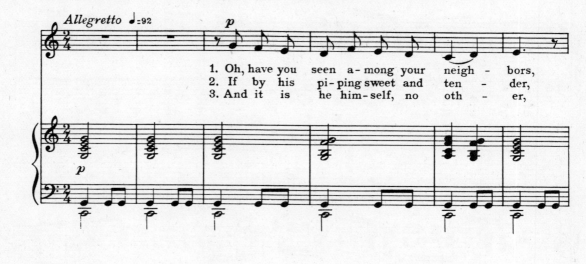

[1] From *The Progressive Music Series*, Book Four, copyright, 1920, by permission of the publishers, Silver Burdett Company, New York.

ways quite to your mind, Who shares with all his love and la-
sings so plain-tive-ly All hearts are rea-dy to sur-ren-
lamb from out the fold, My shep-herd gives both lamb and moth-

bors? Ah! that is Jean! Bring him to me!
der, Ah! that is Jean! Bring him to me!
er; Ah! that is Jean! Bring him to me!

I have his heart,— My faith has he.
I have his heart,— My faith has he.
I have his heart,— My faith has he.

1. Ah! s'il est dans votre village
   Un berger sensible et charmant,
   Qu'on chérisse au premier moment,
   Qu'on aime ensuite davantage

      C'est mon ami,
      rendez-le moi!
      J'ai son amour,
      il a ma foi.

2. Si par sa voix tendre et plaintive
   Il charme l'écho de vos bois.
   Si les accents de son hautbois
   Rendent la bergère pensive,

      C'est encor lui,
      rendez-le moi!
      J'ai son amour,
      il a ma foi.

3. Si passant près de sa chaumière
   Le pauvre en voyant son troupeau,
   Ose demander un agneau
   Et qu'il obtienne encor la mère,

      Oh! c'est bien lui,
      rendez-le moi!
      J'ai son amour,
      il a ma foi.

13 *Larghetto, e piano* (♪=112)  HANDEL (*He Shall Feed His Flock*)

He shall feed His flock like a shep - - herd,

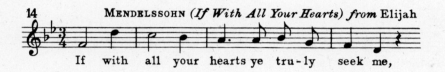

14 MENDELSSOHN (*If With All Your Hearts*) *from* Elijah

If with all your hearts ye tru-ly seek me,

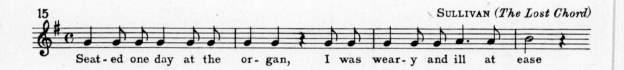

15 SULLIVAN (*The Lost Chord*)

Seat-ed one day at the or-gan, I was wear-y and ill at ease

## QUESTIONS AND ACTIVITIES

1. What is a "phrase?" Illustrate in a sentence and in a musical composition.
2. What does the term "good phrasing" imply?
3. Compare the length of phrases in songs and exercises you can sing easily now with those you were able to perform in beginning lessons.
4. Indicate in the exercises and songs in this lesson where breath might be taken legitimately in case the supply were exhausted before the end of the phrase. Sing them in this manner, then sing them without breaking them. Which is the more effective and why?
5. Give a brief report on the life of Handel and include a list of his compositions with which you are familiar:

## SUPPLEMENTARY LIST OF MUSIC

Unison — Songs My Mother Taught Me — *Dvořák.* B (d#-e), D (f#-g)
S A — Wanderer's Evening Song — *Rubinstein*
S S A — O Can Ye Sew Cushions — *Scotch Song* arr. by *Bantock*
T T B B — On Great Lone Hills — *Sibelius-Matthews*
S A T B — Adoramus Te Christe — *Palestrina*

# 24

## CONTRAST IN TONE

*His voice in one dull, deep unvaried sound,*
*Seems to break forth from caverns underground.*

— Churchill

To express the musical and textual meaning of a song interestingly and effectively, you should be able to produce sounds of different color or timbre and intensity. Usually in even a short song, voice should change in these respects from phrase to phrase. These changes should be made smoothly and freely. Your voice should be musical at all times, neither becoming strained and blatant in loud passages nor repressed and lifeless in soft phrases. Moreover, you should be able to increase and diminish the amount of sound at will, even on a single tone. This is called *messa di voce* (literally "sending of the voice").

The ability to begin a tone softly and gradually and imperceptibly increase its volume, and then to bring it back in the same manner to the same degree of power with which it started, shows correct use of the voice and fine vocal control.

### EXERCISES

Practice with different consonant and vowel combinations such as *mah, fah, nay, noh,* etc. Sing exercises 1–4 according to the markings, then reverse the order.

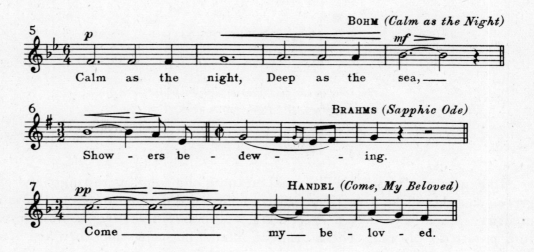

## QUESTIONS AND ACTIVITIES

1. What is meant by the term *messa di voce*?
2. What symbol in music signifies that the *messa di voce* effect is to be employed?
3. List characteristics of an effective *messa di voce*.
4. Why is "The Plane Tree" by Handel a good song in which to use the *messa di voce*?
5. Where may this effect be used legitimately in songs you have sung in previous lessons?

## SUPPLEMENTARY LIST OF MUSIC

Unison — Come Raggio di Sol — *Caldara*.  F mi (d–f), D mi (c#–d)
S A — The Sun Worshippers — *Zuni Indian Song* arr. by *Loomis*
S S A — Good Night, Good Night Beloved — *Pinsuti*
T T B B — Song of the Volga Boatmen — *Russian Folk Song*
S A T B — As Torrents in Summer — *Elgar*

# The Plane Tree

From the opera "Xerxes"

GEORGE FREDERICK HANDEL
(1685–1759)

This aria is sung by the tenor in the first act of the opera, "Xerxes." The scene discloses a garden in which is growing a lovely plane tree. Xerxes appears and sings: " 'Mong all the trees that grow, thou art the loveliest, thou ne'er will fade." The song, generally known today by the term *Largo*, is heard in many arrangements for instruments and voices and with different words, particularly of a religious nature. The sustained tone at the beginning provides good opportunity for the use of the *messa di voce*. In fact, there is frequent opportunity throughout the piece for a variety of dynamic effects. The markings should be carefully observed. The song may be transposed into the keys of E and F at the discretion of the teacher and singer, and the first phrase may be used as a vocalise by singing it in various keys.

# 25

## CHROMATICS

*Rills of music, note on note,*
*Spilling the air with mellow gold.*

— Cawein

In music, there often occur intermediate tones or chromatics to give greater variety and interest to the composition. Sometimes they are used purely as passing or ornamental tones; at other times they serve to take the music from one key or mode into another.

When a succession of chromatics or twelve half-tones are found within the octave the chromatic scale is formed. Songs and exercises containing passages built on this scale or portions of it provide valuable training to students of singing, for by taking the voice through a series of these intervals, purity of intonation and vocal control are developed. In singing rapid chromatic scales and passages, it is sometimes difficult to keep them smooth and at the same time maintain distinctness and accuracy of pitch of every note. Fluent execution is aided if you feel a definite accent in the exercises. It is well to sing them slowly at first, increasing the tempo as you gain skill.

### EXERCISES

* In singing chromatic scales, think of the upward intervals as being large, and coming down the scale, imagine small intervals. This little mental process will help you to sing a chromatic scale in tune. *E. L.*

Tosti (*Good-bye*)

Fall-ing leaf and fad-ing tree, Lines of white in a sul-len sea,
Shad-ows ris-ing on you and me, Shad-ows ris-ing on you and me;

Grieg (*With a Water Lily*)

Wa-ter-nymphs are lost in slum-ber, Lil-ies play in count-less num-ber.

Spohr (*Rose Softly Blooming*)

Liv-ing and dy - - ing Sweet ___ rose, like thee.

## QUESTIONS AND ACTIVITIES

1. How are chromatics or intermediate tones used in musical compositions? Find examples of different methods of using them.
2. How is the chromatic scale constructed?
3. Why is the chromatic scale or songs employing chromatic intervals valuable in developing vocal control?
4. Although both Wagner and Grieg have used many chromatic or intermediate tones in the songs included in this lesson, each has employed them in a different manner and has achieved different effects. Differentiate between the moods of these two songs. How has the use of chromatics helped to secure these effects?
5. Prepare brief biographies of Wagner and Grieg.
6. Tell the story of "Tannhäuser."

### SUPPLEMENTARY LIST OF MUSIC

Unison — Elegie — *Massenet.* E mi (b–f), F mi (c–g♭)
S A — Habanera from "Carmen" — *Bizet* arr. by *Remick*
S S A — Murmuring Zephyrs — *Jensen*
T T B B — Song of India — *Rimsky-Korsakoff*
S A T B - - Pilgrims' Chorus from "Tannhäuser" — *Wagner*

# Song to the Evening Star

From the opera "Tannhäuser"

RICHARD WAGNER
(1813–1883)

Richard Wagner stands as a supreme genius in the field of dramatic music. Not only was he richly endowed musically, but he was also gifted in literature and painting. He wrote his own libretti and acted as his own stage manager, costume and mechanical designer. Hence his music dramas are entirely his own and show unity of subject, language, music, action, and setting.

The opera "Tannhäuser," from which "Song to the Evening Star" is taken, is based on both legend and fact about the minstrel minnesinger knights of the medieval ages. The song appears in the third act. Wolfram has been listening to the chant of the pilgrims on their return from Rome. As the sound dies away, he looks up and beholds the evening star. Inspired by this symbol of hope, he takes his harp and improvises this song. To appreciate its full significance, the story of the opera should be read.

This aria should be sung slowly and quietly. The first and last phrases may be used as exercises in various keys, for they are excellent studies for developing breath control and vocal flexibility.

from_____ a - far. With glow-ing heart that ne'er_____ dis-
dich_____ so gern; vom Her - zen, das sie nie_____ ver-

closed, Greet her when she in thy light_____ re-posed.
rieth, grü - sse sie, wenn sie vor-bei_____ dir zieht,

When part-ing from this vale_____ a vis - ion, She ris - es
wenn sie ent-schwebt dem Thal_____ der Er - den, ein sel' - ger

to_____ an an - gel's mis - sion; When part - ing from this
En - gel dort_____ zu wer - den, wenn sie ent-schwebt dem

p un poco ritard.

vale\_\_\_ a vis - ion She ris - es to an_____
*Thal\_\_\_ der Er - den, ein sel' - ger En - gel_____*

an - gel's mis - sion.
*dort\_\_\_ zu wer - den.*

# The First Primrose

J. Paulsen
English version by Frederick Corder

Edvard Hagerup Grieg
(1843-1907)

This delicate, graceful song by Norway's most characteristic composer tells about the delight which the primrose brings as the first token of spring after the long, dreary Scandinavian winter. It should be sung with flowing, flexible rhythm and cheerful tone. Because of many chromatic intervals, this song is a good test of a singer's accuracy of intonation.

Oh, take, thou love-ly child of Spring, This Spring's first ten-der flow-er, Des-pise it not, that la-ter on Fair ro-ses June will show-er. The sum-mer has its gold-en charm, In au-tumn, hearts are gay, But

Spring is lov-li - er than all, The time of love and play. For thee and me, O dear-est maid, The light of Spring is glow-ing; Then take the flow'r and rap - ture yield, Thy heart on me be - stow-ing.

# 26

## EMBELLISHMENTS

*A plaining song plain singing voice require,*
*For warbling notes from inward cheering flow.*

— Sidney

Tones added to the essential or principal notes of a melody for decorative or other purposes are called embellishments or ornamental tones. They became numerous and prominent in music as early as the sixteenth century. No doubt a reason for their popularity was that early keyboard instruments lacked the sustaining power of our modern piano. In addition, ornamental tones gave opportunity for a display of vocal dexterity in vogue at that time.

As instruments developed and styles of compositions changed so also have forms and use of embellishing notes altered. Formerly they were indicated by the use of small type and by special signs, but in music of the present they usually appear in regular print and are written out in full in the exact time in which the composer wishes them performed. Note the gruppetto written out on page 180.

However, because you will sing music written in previous centuries, you should learn to identify the different groups of notes that compose the older figurations and the signs that stand for them.[1] The manner in which you perform them depends to a great extent, not only upon how they appear in the music, but upon the general character of the composition. Tempo, time value of the ornamental and principal notes, rhythm, and mood should be considered. In most cases your musical taste will guide you.

---

[1] See a standard dictionary or encyclopedia of music for more detailed discussion.
See also Dolmetsch, Arnold. *The Interpretation of the Music of the XVIIth and XVIIIth Centuries.* London, Novello and Company Limited (n.d.). *E. L.*

# 27

## THE APPOGGIATURA

*A few can touch the magic string*
*And noisy fame is proud to win them,*
*Alas for those who never sing*
*But die with all their music in them.*

— Holmes

The appoggiatura (also called *grace* note) comes from an Italian word meaning "to lean upon." It consists of an accented ornamental tone introduced before a principal note of the melody. Time to perform it is taken from the note against which it is printed. No rule as to exact rendition is generally accepted. Some musicians give it its printed value and shorten the next note by the same amount. Others say that the time should be divided equally between it and the note which follows. Sometimes the appoggiatura is allowed to take the major portion of the time if, by chance, the main note is followed by another of the same pitch. Before a dotted note, the appoggiatura is usually given two-thirds of the total value.

A short appoggiatura, also called acciacatura, occurs frequently and is written like the long appoggiatura except that it has a diagonal line through the flag or stem. The name *acciacatura*, from the Italian word meaning "to crush," is definitive, for this embellishment is sung as quickly as possible, being literally pressed into the following note. Time to sing it is taken from the following note, but, unlike the long appoggiatura, it is unaccented.

EXERCISES

# My Mother Bids Me Bind My Hair

Franz Joseph Haydn
(1732–1809)

"Papa" Haydn, affectionately known as the father of the symphony, was not too busy with instrumental music to devote time to vocal music. To this field he made significant contributions, particularly in the larger forms. Among these are masses, motets, cantatas, and oratorios, chief of which are *The Creation* and *The Seasons*.

His song "My Mother Bids Me Bind My Hair" is a good example of the style of lyric writing at that time. The melody is graceful and melodious; the accompaniment is attractive and interesting; the words are vocal and typical of the period. The composition contains good examples of the long form of the appoggiatura. In each case they should be sung lightly, smoothly, and in correct tempo. Breath should be suspended during the rests in the second section of the song. The interpretation should be simple and unaffected, in keeping with the quality of the music and expressive of the sentiment of a young maiden longing for her lover.

hue,           Tie  up___  my sleeves with rib - bands rare,    And

near!           I  sit___  up - on  this mos - sy  stone,    And

lace my bod - ice blue;          Tie up__ my sleeves with rib - bands

sigh when none can hear;         I  sit__ up - on  this mos - sy

rare, And lace, and lace   my bod - ice blue.        "For

stone, And sigh, and sigh  when none can hear.       And

why," she cries, "sit  still  and weep, While oth - ers dance and

while  I  spin  my  flax - en thread, And sing  my sim - ple

EXERCISES

# On Wings of Song

Heinrich Heine

Felix Mendelssohn-Bartholdy
(1809–1847)

Musicians appreciate Mendelssohn's genius. Once it was the vogue to belittle his music because it cannot be classed as "profound."

Like Mendelssohn's nature, his music reflects lightness and joy. It is bright, sparkling, smoothly polished and elegant, never tragic, crude, or introspective. There are seldom shadows, valleys, or dark or rugged paths. No better example of his lyric writing can be found than "On Wings of Song" with its lovely melody and its harp-like accompaniment. A sustained, pure tone and clear diction are necessary for a satisfactory rendition. The coda of five measures is in a deeply contemplative mood. The prolonged E-flat gives opportunity for increasing and diminishing the volume of tone, or the *messa di voce*. The use of the short appoggiatura, or acciacatura, is well illustrated in this composition. They should be sung lightly and accurately.

From *The Progressive Music Series*, Book Four, copyright, 1920, by permission of the publishers, Silver Burdett Company, New York.

see their sis - ter dear.
on,'thou'lt hear him well.

2. There

D.S.

3. Be - neath a broad palm we'll rest us;

Free from the world we'll seem; Re - joiced that fate has

blessed us With such a hap - py dream. Oh, hap - py dream, hap - py dream! Oh, hap - py dream!

# Caro Mio Ben

Giuseppi Giordani
(1744-1798)

The renaissance of music in Italy also expressed itself in the field of opera. Soon the particular style influenced the composition and production of opera in every country in Europe. The Italian "aria" became the means of displaying the vocal art of the singer. Giordani wrote operas and oratorios in this era.

Among the many compositions in this form is the famous and ever popular song "Caro Mio Ben." Embellishing tones are used skillfully throughout and add considerable interest to the simple, yet lovely melody. This is an excellent composition for study of pure, smooth tone production and good phrasing. Indeed, many artists use it as an opening number of a group to display their *bel canto* style and to get the voice in readiness for other songs.

Because Italian is filled with pure vowel sounds, every singer should master the language not only to sing songs with the original text, but also to develop beauty of tone quality.

Dear - est, be - lieve, When - e'er we part; Lone - ly I
*Ca - ro mio ben cre - di - mi al - men sen - za di*

grieve, In my sad heart! When - e'er we
*te lan - gui - sce il cor. Ca - ro mio*

part; Lone-ly I grieve, In my sad heart!
*ben sen - za di te lan - gui - sce il cor.*

Thy faith-ful slave, Lan-guish-ing sighs; Haste then and save Him ere he
*Il tuo fe - del so - spi-ra o - gnor ces - sa cru-del tan-to ri-*

dies! Haste then and save, Haste then and save Him ere he
*gor. Ces - sa cru-del tan - to ri - gor tan - to ri -*

dies! Dear-est, be-lieve, When-e'er we part; Lone-ly I
gor. Ca - ro mio ben cre-di-mial-men sen-za di

grieve, In — my — sad — heart! Dear-est, be - lieve, When-e'er we
te— lan - gui-sce il cor. Ca - ro mio ben cre - di-mial-

part; Lone-ly I grieve,— In my sad heart!
men; sen-za di te — lan - gui-sce il cor.

# 28

## THE GRUPPETTO OR TURN

*Call in sweet music, I have heard soft airs,*
*Can charm our senses and expel our cares.*

— Denham

The gruppetto (indicated by the sign ∾) derived its name from the fact that it twines about its principal note. The usual form consists of four notes: first the tone above the principal one; second, the principal note; third, the tone below it, and fourth, the principal tone again. In the inverted turn, the order is reversed, the tone below the main one being performed first.

When the sign (∾) appears over a note of small value in fast tempo the turn is comprised of four tones of equal length; when it occurs over a note of greater value in slow tempo the first tones are usually sung quickly and the fourth is held until the time value of the note has expired. If the turn sign is placed to the right of the note, it is held almost to the full time-value, then the turn is sung just before the next tone of the melody.

A chromatic sign over or under the turn signifies that the highest or lowest note of the turn is to be altered accordingly.

### EXERCISES

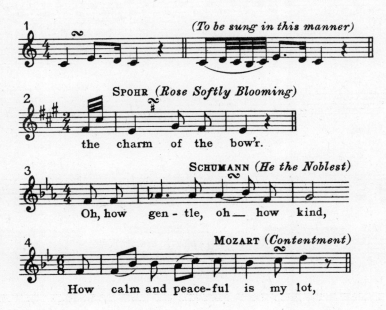

# Faith in Spring

FRANZ SCHUBERT
(1797-1828)

In this setting of Ludwig Uhland's poem, Schubert displays anew his genius for effecting a perfect union of text and music. Both voice the freshness and beauty of spring. Schubert used appoggiaturas and turns throughout the composition to obtain the desired effects of lightness and delicacy. The measures containing these musical embellishments may be transposed into other keys and sung with different vowel sounds and syllables as well as the printed words for they are valuable aids in training the voice.

The English translation is also from "Rosamunde." (See page 139.)

heart - beat swells,          With  Spring comes new     life,
get       thy gloom,          With  Spring comes new     life,

new_____ life glow - ing,      With Spring comes    new___ life,
new_____ life glow - ing,      With Spring comes    new___ life,

new  life_ glow -       - ing.
new  life_ glow -       - ing.

# 29

## THE MORDENT AND THE TRILL

*Song brings of itself a cheerfulness that wakes
the soul to joy.*

— Euripides

The term *mordent* (indicated by the sign ✷) is taken from the French word *mordre* meaning "to bite." It was applied probably because the ornament is really a part of the trill. It consists usually of three tones: first, the one represented by the printed note; second, the one below it; and third, the printed note or tone of departure. In the inverted mordent (indicated by the sign ∿) the note above a printed one is sung rather than the one below. A double or long mordent has five or seven tones instead of three. In all cases, the embellishment should be quickly sung with the chief note carrying the accent.

The trill ( 𝄊 ) is a rapid alternation of two notes to the full value of the printed one. A perfect trill closes with a turn. Although you may not encounter the trill often in the songs you sing nor possibly may not be able to perform it as quickly and perfectly as it should be, yet you should know what it is and through practicing it realize to some degree the finely attuned mechanism it takes to sing it well.

EXERCISES

—— 181 ——

## QUESTIONS AND ACTIVITIES

1. What are embellishments or ornamental tones in music?
2. Name and explain forms or kinds commonly found.
3. Give probable reasons for the popularity of embellishing tones in songs composed in the seventeenth and eighteenth centuries.
4. Illustrate ways of writing or indicating ornamental notes.
5. Why is it important for you to know how to identify the different figurations and the signs that stand for them?
6. Enumerate points that should be considered in singing embellishing tones.
7. Analyze all the songs you have studied thus far for embellishing notes.
8. Report briefly on Haydn's contribution to music.
9. How did Italian opera influence the production of native opera in Germany, France, and England in the seventeenth, eighteenth, and nineteenth centuries?

## SUPPLEMENTARY LIST OF MUSIC

Unison — The Slighted Swain — *Old English Melody.* G (c–d), B♭ (e♭–f)
S A — I Know a Bank — *Horn*
S S A — Happy Childhood from "Figaro" — *Mozart* arr. by *Page*
T T B B — O Sole Mio — *di Capua*
S A T B — Sleep While the Soft Evening Breezes — *Bishop*

# Damon

MAX STANGE

Max Stange, a contemporary German composer, has set Goethe's romantic poem to music in a manner admirably suited to the reminiscent thoughts of a young girl as she wanders through the woods.

This song should be sung gracefully and simply with smooth, pure tone. The various nuances of expression necessary for an interesting rendition are indicated in the score and should be observed. The refrain is a good exercise in flexibility and may be used as such by transposing it into various keys.

As I roam'd the woods at lei - sure In the
Bei dem Glanz der A - bend - rö - the ging ich

eve - ning hour so still, Da - mon
still den Wald ent - lang, Da - mon

sat and piped for plea - sure, Ech - o an - swer'd from the
sass und blies die Flö - te, dass es von den Fel - sen

lay - ing,  Kissed me soft - ly looked and sighed;
nie - der,  küss - te mich so hold und süss,

But I bade him
und ich sag - te:

still be play - ing, And the kind - ly youth com - plied: so
bla - se wie - der, und der gu - te Jun - ge blies: so

la re la

la     la _____     la

la _____

*poco rubato*

*mf*

*tr ad lib.*

*poco più lento*

*rit.*

*poco più lento*

Now, a - las,   I   wan - der lone - ly,   All ___ my
*Mei - ne Ruh' ist   nun ver - lo - ren, mei - ne*

*cresc.*

joy   is   turn'd to pain,                    Dream - ing, wak - ing,
*Freu - de   floh da - von,                    und ___ ich hör' vor*

*p*

*cresc.*

hear__ I on__ly Da - mon's sweet and ten - der strain,
_mei__ nen Oh__ ren im__ mer nur den al - ten Ton:_

so la__

re la__ la la__

la la.

# Verdant Meadows

GEORGE FREDERICK HANDEL
(1685–1759)

In Handel's time all singers were expected to have the skill necessary to sing the florid arias in the Italian style which were the vogue in England as well as on the continent. Even in the most dignified and sustained types of compositions vocal embellishments were used, especially at the cadences. The aria "Verdant Meadows," from "Alcina," is an example of such style of composition.

If desired, the trills may be omitted and the mordent may be substituted for them.

Ver - dant mead-ows, for-est shad-ows,
Ver - di pra-ti sel-ve_a - me - ne,

All _____ your bloom will pass ___ a - way;
Per - de - re-te la bel - tà.

Purl - ing streams, flow'rs fresh - ly glow - ing,
*Va - ghi fior, cor - ren - ti ri - vi,*

All your beau - ty swift - ly go - ing,
*La va - ghez - za, la bel - lez - za,*

Seem-eth fair but for a day.
*Pre - sto in voi si can - ge - rà.*

Ver - dant mead-ows, for - est shad - ows,
*Ver - di pra - ti sel - ve a - me - ne,*

mead - ows, for - est shad - ows, Ye are 
*pra - ti sel - ve a - me - ne, Per - de -*

fair but for a day; All must die and
*re - te la bel - tà, Per - de - re - te*

*colla voce*

fade a - way.
*la bel - tà.*

*p*

*p*   *mf*

# Nina

Giovanni Battiste Pergolesi
(1710–1736)

Opera bouffe, that is, comic opera, is said to have originated with Giovanni Battiste Pergolesi, an exceptional genius of the Neapolitan School that flourished in the early eighteenth century. His opera "La Serva Padrona" is the first great example in this style and is still popular in Italian and English versions. An unhappy love affair and ill health tinged many of his songs with sadness. The air, Nina, discloses his ability to portray this mood.

The singer should pay careful attention to change of moods and styles within the piece. The interval of a second, which is often incorrectly produced, occurs frequently. Think this succession of tones as a larger step in ascending passages and smaller in descending to insure true intonation. Attack each tone accurately and avoid the use of portamento, especially in the octave skips.

If the English translation is used, it is well to retain the Italian pronunciation of *Nina* (*i* as in *machine*, not *i* as in *sigh*).

net - ta!     A - wak - en, O Ni - net - ta!     A - wak - en, O Ni -
net - ta,     sve - glia - te, mia Ni - net - ta,     ac - cio non dor - ma

net - ta, A - wake nor slum - ber more!     A - wak - en, O Ni -
più,     ac - cio non dor - ma più:     Sve - glia - te, mia Ni -

*pp*

*ossia*

net - ta, A - wak - en O Ni - net - ta, A - wake! nor slum - ber
net - ta, sve - glia - te, mia Ni - net - ta, ac - cio non dor - ma

*pp*

**1.**     **2.**     *f*     *a piacere*

more.     more, A - wake! nor slum - ber more!
più.     più, ac - cio non dor - ma più.

*f*     *dim.*     *pp colla voce*

# REFERENCE BOOKS

Annesley, Charles. *The Standard Opera Glass.* Brentano's, New York, 1931

Bauer, Marion, and Peyser, Ethel R. *Music Through the Ages.* G. P. Putnam's Sons, New York, 1932

Dole, Nathan Haskell. *Famous Composers.* Thomas Y. Crowell Company, New York, 1929

Ewen, David. *Composers of Today.* H. W. Wilson Company, New York, 1934
Ewen, David. *Composers of Yesterday.* H. W. Wilson Company, New York, 1937

Finck, Henry T. *Songs and Song Writers.* Charles Scribner's Sons, New York, 1923
Finney, Theodore Mitchell. *A History of Music.* Harcourt, Brace and Company, New York, 1935

Grove, Sir George. *Dictionary of Music.* The Macmillan Company, New York, 1927

Hamilton, Clarence G. *Outlines of Music History.* Oliver Ditson Company, Boston, 1924
Howard, John Tasker. *Our American Music.* Thomas Y. Crowell, New York, 1931

Kobbé, Gustav. *The Complete Opera Book.* G. P. Putnam's Sons, New York, 1935
Kolodin, Irving. *The Metropolitan Opera, 1883-1935.* Oxford University Press, New York, 1936

McConathy, Osbourne, Embs, Anton H., Howes, Maude M., and Fouser, Charles E. *An Approach to Harmony.* Silver Burdett Company, New York, 1927

Pratt, Waldo Selden, Editor. *The New Encyclopedia of Music and Musicians.* The Macmillan Company, New York, 1929

Thompson, Oscar. *The American Singer, A Hundred Years of Success in Opera.* The Dial Press, New York, 1937

White, Bernice, and Jones, Vincent. *Harmonic Dictation.* American Book Company, New York, 1932

# APPENDIX

## A. FOREIGN LANGUAGES

The following pronunciation keys are intended to serve only as guides to the student in the correct formation of sounds. They are by no means adequate to teach him the intricacies and peculiarities of each language. In so far as possible, sounds are explained by comparison with English, but it should be borne in mind that the sounds of any two languages are rarely identical. The general rule for pronunciation of any sound or combination of sounds is given, but there are often exceptions. Therefore, it is always advisable to refer to a standard pronouncing dictionary, or, better still, to study the language with a competent teacher.

### ITALIAN

#### Vowels

Italian vowels are pronounced with a full, clear sound. They never should become diphthongal in quality.

| Italian symbol | Approximate sound represented in English words |
|---|---|
| *a* | father |
| *e* close | fate |
| *e* open | bell |
| *i* | see |
| *o* close | tone |
| *o* open | saw |
| *u* | boot |

#### Consonants

The letters *k*, *w*, *x*, and *y* do not occur in modern Italian. Otherwise the alphabet is the same as in English. Only the sounds that depart from the usual pronunciation in English will be described.

| | |
|---|---|
| *c* | Before *e* or *i*, this symbol has the sound of *ch* in *chin;* elsewhere it is like English *k* as in *key.* |
| *g* | Before *e* or *i*, it has the sound of *g* in *gem;* elsewhere, like *g* as in *go.* |

| Italian symbol | Approximate sound represented in English words |
|---|---|
| *h* | This consonant is not sounded. |
| *j* | Like *y* in *yes* |
| *n* | Before *q* or hard *c* (*k*), this consonant has the sound of English *ng*. |
| *s* | As an initial sound, *s* is pronounced like *s* in *see*. Between two vowels it generally has the sound of *s* in *rose*. |
| *z* | A single *z* or a double *zz* is pronounced *ts* and sometimes *dz*. |

#### Combinations of Consonants

| | |
|---|---|
| *ch* | *k* |
| *gh* | Like *g* in *go*. |
| *sch* | Like *sk* in *skate*. |
| *gl* | If followed by the vowel *i*, this combination resembles *lli* in *million*. |
| *gn* | This combination is usually pronounced like *ni* in *opinion*. |
| *qu* | Like *qu* in *quick* |
| *sc* | Before *e* and *i*, the sound is like *sh* in *ship*. Before other vowels, the sound is *sk*. |

### GERMAN

#### Vowels

General Rules:

Vowels are either short or long.

a. A vowel is usually short before two consonants. However, a long root sound is retained before affixes.

b. A vowel is long when ending a syllable. It is usually long when followed by one consonant.

c. A vowel followed by *h* in the same syllable is long.

d. A double vowel is long.

| German symbol | Approximate sound represented in English words |
|---|---|
| *a* long | father |
| *a* short | similar to long sound but of shorter duration |
| *ä* long | dare |
| *ä* short | met |
| *e* long | they |
| *e* short | bell |

# APPENDIX

## GERMAN (Cont'd)

### Vowels

| German symbol | Approximate sound represented in English words |
|---|---|
| | In monosyllabic prefixes and unaccented suffixes, *e* short is similar in sound to the English vowel in *it* or the sound represented by *e* in *deny*. As the final letter of a word, it has a weak sound as in the English definite article *the*. Final *en* is pronounced like *en* in *sudden*. |
| *i* long | see |
| *i* short | it |
| *ie* | see |
| *o* long | tone |
| *o* short | nut |
| *ö* long | Has no counterpart in English. It is produced by rounding the lips as if to produce *o* as in *no* with the tongue in position for *a* as in *say*. |
| *ö* short | Resembles somewhat the sound *er* in *mercy* when pronounced with lips well rounded. |
| *u* long | rule |
| *u* short | pull |
| *ü* long | Has no English equivalent. It is formed by rounding the lips as when saying *oo* in *good* with the tongue in position for *ee* as in *see*. |
| *ü* short | Is formed in the same way as *ü* long, but is uttered quickly. |

### Diphthongs

All diphthongs are long.

| | |
|---|---|
| *ae* | dare |
| *ai* | aisle |
| *au* | house |
| *äu* | boy |
| *ei* ⎫ | |
| *ey* ⎭ | my |
| *eu* | boy |
| *oi* | boy |
| *ui* | wee |

### Consonants

As a rule, the German language has no silent consonant, except *h* which is an aspirate sound. Only those sounds which depart from the usual English pronunciation will be described.

| German symbol | Approximate sound represented in English words |
|---|---|
| *b, d* | As in *be, do*. When these sounds occur at the end of a word or at the end of a syllable preceding another consonant, they are pronounced *p*, and *t*, respectively. |
| *c* | Before *ei, i, y, ä, ö*, this symbol is pronounced like *ts*. |
| *g* | When the initial sound and when doubled, *g* is pronounced as in *go*. At the end of a word or when it occurs before another consonant, it sometimes has a guttural or breathed sound. |
| *h* | As in *he*. In connection with some sounds, as for example *t* (*th*), it is silent. |
| *j* | *y* as in *yes*. |
| *s* | When final, or when doubled or preceding another consonant, *s* is pronounced as in *so*. In other cases it has the sound of *z* in *zeal*, or *s* in *rose*. |
| *w* | *v* as in *very*. |
| *x* | *ks* |
| *z* | *ts* |
| *ch* | This combination of consonants represents a guttural or a breathed sound. The tongue is raised toward the roof of the mouth as if saying *k* and the breath is allowed to escape gradually and not in an explosive puff as in English. |
| *chs* | When this combination of consonants forms a part of the root of the word, it is pronounced *ks*. When *s* belongs to another part of the word, it is pronounced separately and *ch* as above. |

## GERMAN (Cont'd)

| German symbol | Approximate sound represented in English words | German symbol | Approximate sound represented in English words |
|---|---|---|---|
| ck | k | sch | sh (when in the same syllable) |
| kn | k and n (sounded separately) | sc | sk (usually) |
| ng | Like ng in sing when in the same syllable. | st, sp | At the beginning of a word st is pronounced sht and sp has the sound shp. In the middle or at the end of a word they are pronounced as in English (lest, list). |
| th | Like t in to. | | |
| pf | p and f (sounded separately) | | |
| ph | f | | |

## FRENCH

### Vowels

In pronouncing French vowels, never drawl them so that they become diphthongs. In every case, they should be uniform throughout their utterance. The student, therefore, should be careful not to change the position of his tongue or lips during the prolongation of sound.

| French symbol | Approximate sound represented in English words |
|---|---|
| a, à | dance |
| â | father |
| é | say |
| è, ê | bell |
| e | the; or o in of |
| i, î | see |
| ô | note; no |
| o | not |
| u, û | This symbol has no English equivalent. It is made by rounding the lips as when saying oo in tool with the tongue in position for ee as in see. |
| y | When beginning a syllable and used as a consonant y has the sound of y in yes; when not beginning a syllable it takes on the nature of a vowel and is pronounced like ee as in see. |
| ai, aî | met |
| au, eau | no |
| ei | let |
| eu, eû, oeu | For such combinations of vowel sounds, the lips should be closely rounded as when saying oo as in good and the tongue should have the position as when saying a as in say. |
| ou, où, oú | boot |

### Nasal Vowels

Nasal vowels have no English equivalents. They are formed by saying the French vowel and at the same time allowing the breath to escape through the nose. It should be noted that there is no sound of m, n, or ng in French nasal vowels. Therefore, the student must exercise great care not to change the position of the tongue or velum, nor to close the lips, until the sound is complete.

The sign of nasality is a single m or n in the same syllable with the vowel. But if m or n is followed by a vowel, or is doubled, or if mn occurs, there is regularly no nasality.

### Consonants

Only the sounds that depart from the usual English pronunciation will be described.

| | |
|---|---|
| c | Before a, o, u or a consonant or when final, c has the sound of k as in key. Before e, i, y it is pronounced like s as in see. When the cedilla is used (ç) the sound is always s as in see. |
| ch | Like sh in show. |
| g | Before a, o, u, or a consonant, g is pronounced as in go. Before e, i, y it is similar in sound to s in measure. |
| gn | This combination of sounds is pronounced somewhat like ni in opinion. |
| q, qu | Like k in key. |
| s | As in see; rose. |
| sc | Like sc in scene. |
| th | Like t in to. |
| w | This symbol is usually sounded like v as in very |
| z | As in zone. |

## B.  ADDITIONAL LIST OF SONGS FOR SOLO VOICES AND ENSEMBLE GROUPS

The compass of each song is indicated by large and small letters, the first letter showing the lowest and the second the highest notes.  Small letters represent notes appearing on the staff, capital letters are used for notes above or below the staff.

Because many of the compositions given here are appropriate for different types of voices, various keys of the songs are listed. Under Soprano and Tenor the highest key appears first while under Contralto and Bass the lowest key is recorded first.

### Soprano

Arne, *Where the Bee Sucks*  G(d-G), F(C-f)

Becker, *Springtide*  A(e-A), G(D-G), Fb(C-f)
Besley, *The Second Minuet*  Bb(f-f), G(d-d)
Brogi, *Lullaby*  G(d-G), Eb(Bb-eb)
Brownell, *The Four-Leaf Clover*  G(D-G), F(C-f), Eb(Bb-eb)

Cadman, *From the Land of the Sky Blue Water*  Bb(f-f), Ab(eb-eb), Gb(db-db), Eb(Bb-bb)
Carew, *Tip-toe*  Eb(eb-G), C(C-e)
Curran, *Ho! Mr. Piper*  F(d-G), D(B-e)

DeKoven, *A Winter Lullaby*  Bb(f-f), Ab(eb-eb)

Foote, *Irish Folk Song*  Gmi(D-G), Emi(B-e)

Godard, *Berceuse*  Gmi(f-G), Fmi(eb-f)
Goodhart, *A Fairy Went a-Marketing*  A(d-e), F(Bb-c)
Gretchaninoff, *Slumber Song*  E(D-G#), C(B-e)
Gretchaninoff, *The Snow Drop*  F(c-G), Eb(B-f)

Horn, *I've Been Roaming*  F(e-A), Eb(d-G), C(B-e)
Huerter, *Pirate Dreams*  Ab(eb-Ab), Gb(Db-Gb)

Lehmann, *Good-morning, Brother Sunshine*  Eb(eb-Ab), C(C-f), A(A-d)

Mozart, *Lullaby*  G(g-G), F(f-f)

Needham, *Husheen*  D(D-f#), C(C-e), Bb(Bb-d)

Reger, *The Virgin's Slumber Song*  Ab(eb-Ab), F(C-f), Eb(Bb-eb)
Ronald, *Sunbeams*  Eb(d-G), D(C#-f#), C(B-e)

Salter, *Come to the Garden, Love*  Eb(eb-Ab), C(C-f)
Schneider, *Flower Rain*  Bb(f-A), Gb(db-f)
Strickland, *My Lover is a Fisherman*  Bb(d-G), G(B-e)

Tosti, *Serenade*  F(e-f), Eb(d-eb), C(B-c)

# ADDITIONAL LIST OF SONGS

## Contralto

Bemberg, *Hindoo Song,* Gmi(C-eb), Ami(D-f), Bmi(e-G)

Cadman, *As in a Rose Jar* C(A-c), Eb(C-eb), F(d-f)
Cadman, *At Dawning* E(B-d#), Gb(Db-f), Ab(eb-G)
Calbreath, *My Love Rode By* Eb(Bb-eb), F(C-f)

Grinnell, *Behave Yourself Before Folk* F(C-d), G(D-e), Bb(f-G)

Hahn, *Were My Song With Wings Provided* C(A-e), D(B-f#), E(c#-G#)
Hawley, *Daisies* Eb(Bb-d), G(D-f)
Hazelhurst, *O Leave Your Sheep* Eb(Bb-eb), F(c-f), G(d-G)
Head, *The Ships of Arcady* Bb(Bb-eb), D(D-G)
Hildach, *In My Native Village* E(B-e), G(D-G)
Hildach, *My Lover is a Weaver* E(B-e), F(C-f), G(D-G)

Irish Folk Song, *Over the Hills and Far Away* Emi(B-e), Gmi(d-G)

Jensen, *Press Thy Cheek Against Mine Own* Db(Bb-db), Eb(C-eb)

Kountz, *Prayer of the Norwegian Child* Fmi(C-e)

Leoni, *The Birth of Morn,* Eb(eb-eb), F(f-f), G(g-g)

Nevin, *A Necklace of Love* E(B-c#)

Riego, del, *Slave Song* Dmi(C#-d), Emi(d#-e), Fmi(e-f), Gmi(f#-G)
Ronald, *O Lovely Night* Bb(A-d), Db(C-f)

Scott, *Lullaby* Db(Bb-db), Eb(C-eb), F(D-f)
Speaks, *In Maytime* C(D-e), Eb(f-G)

Ware, *Boat Song* D(A-d), F(C-f), G(D-G)
Weatherly, *Danny Boy* D(A-d), F(C-f), G(D-G)
Whelpley, *The Nightingale Has a Lyre of Gold* B(C#-d#), Db(eb-f), E(f#-G#)
Woodman *Ashes of Roses* C#mi(C#-c#), F#mi(f#-f#)
Woodman, *In Arcady* G(D-e)

## Tenor

Aylward, *Beloved, It is Morn* F(f-f), D(d-d), C(C-c)

Beethoven, *I Love Thee* G(D-f)

Cadman, *The Little Road to Kerry* G(D-G), Eb(Bb-eb)
Chadwick, *Allah* E(c#-G#), Db(Bb-f)
Chadwick, *Thou Art So Like a Flower* E(e-G#), Db(db-f)
Clay, *I'll Sing Thee Songs of Araby* Ab(eb-Ab), F(C-f)
Coombs, *Her Rose* C(f#-G), Ab(d-eb)

English Folk Song, *When Love is Kind* Ab(eb-Ab), F(C-f)

# APPENDIX

Fontenailles, *A Resolve*  Db(eb-Gb), B(C#-e)

Ganz, *A Memory*  G(e-G), D(B-d)
German, *Charming Chloe*  F(e-G)

Higgins, *My Lovely Celia*  Ab(eb-f), F(C-d)

Irish Folk Song, *Down by the Sally Gardens*  E(e-f#), C(C-d)

Kountz, *The Sleigh*  Fmi(f-f), Dmi(d-d)

Lieurance, *By the Waters of Minnetonka*  A(e-f#), Gb(db-eb)
Löhr, *The Little Irish Girl*  D(d-f#), C(C-e), Bb(Bb-d)

MacDowell, *Thy Beaming Eyes*,  F(C-f), Eb(Bb-eb)
McGill, *Duna*  Eb(eb-G), Db(Db-f), C(C-e)
Martin, *Come to the Fair*  C(g-G), Bb(f-f), A(e-e), G(d-d)

Nelson, *Mary of Argyle*  G(e-f#)

Quilter, *Now Sleeps the Crimson Petal*  Gb(eb-Gb), F(D-f), Eb(C-eb), D(B-d)

Rogers, *At Parting*  F#(C#-f#), D(A-d)

Speaks, *My Homeland*,  C(f-G), Bb(eb-f), Ab(Db-eb)
Stanford, *Trottin' to the Fair*,  F(e-G), Eb(D-f), D(C#-e), C(B-d)

Taylor, *May-Day Carol*  Eb(d-G), Db(C-f)

## Baritone and Bass

Carissimi, *Victoria, Victoria*  B(B-e), C(C-f), D(d-G)

Dix, *The Trumpeter*  F(A-c), G(B-d), A(C#-e), C(e-G)

Flegier, *The Horn*  F(f-f)
Foote, *I'm Wearing Awa' to the Land o' the Leal*  Bb(Bb-d), Db(db-f)
Forsyth, *Tell Me Not of a Lovely Lass*  C(C-e)

Galloway, *The Gypsy Trail*  F(C-d), A(e-f)
German, *Rolling Down to Rio*  Gmi(G-d), Ami(A-e)

Homer, *A Banjo Song*  A(C#-d), C(e-f)

Keel, *Trade Winds*  Eb(Bb-eb), G(d-G)
Kernochan, *Smuggler's Song*  Dmi(C#-eb)

Lang, *An Irish Folk Song*  D(A-e), F(C-G)
Leoni, *Tally-Ho*  D(C#-d), F(e-f)
Lully, arr. by A. L., *Bois Epais* (Sombre Woods)  Eb(C-eb), F(d-f)

# ADDITIONAL LIST OF SONGS

Margetson, *Tommy Lad*  C(A-d), D(B-e), Eb(C-f), F(d-G)

O'Hara, *Give a Man a Horse He Can Ride*  G(G-b), Bb(Bb-d), D(d-f#)

Robinson, *Water Boy*  D(d-d)
Roeckel, *Happy Three*  Bb(Bb-d)
Rogers, *Sea Fever*  Dmi(d-d), Emi(e-e)

Sanderson, *Shipmates o'Mine*  F(G-d), G(A-e)
Sanderson, *Susan is Her Name O*  G(d-e), Bb(f-G)
Schumann, *The Two Grenadiers*  Gmi(A-d), Bmi(C#-f#)
Secchi, *Love Me or Not*  E(B-e), G(d-G)
Secchi, *Lungi dal Caro Bene* (When Two that Love are Parted) Db(Ab-f), D(A-f#)
Speaks, *Sylvia*  Db(Ab-db), Eb(Bb-eb), F(C-f), G(d-G)
Strickland, *The Road to Home*, Eb(Bb-eb), G(d-G)

Wilson, *False Phyllis*  A(A-d), C(C-f)
Woodforde-Finden, *Kashmiri Song*  Bb(Bb-d), C(C-e), D(d-f#), F(f-A)

## SACRED SOLOS

Ashford, *My Task*  F(e-f), Eb(d-eb), D(C#-d)

Bartlett, *O Lord Be Merciful*  D(d-A), C(C-G)
Burnham, *Jerusalem the Golden*  A(e-G), F(C-e)

Chadwick, *Hark, Hark My Soul*  Db(C-A), Bb(A-Gb)
Coenen, *Come Unto Me*  F(eb-f), D(C-d)
Crowninshield, *There is a Land Mine Eye Hath Seen*  G(d-G), Eb(Bb-eb)

Dennée, *Easter Song*  Eb(eb-G), C(C-e)
Diack, *All in the April Evening*  Fmi(db-G), Dmi(Bb-e), Cmi(Ab-d)
Doun, *Father in Heaven*  Eb(eb-f), C(C-d)

Gaines, *Father of Love*  D(C-e)
Gounod, *The King of Love My Shepherd Is*  F(e-G), D(C#-e), C(B-d)
Gounod, *There is a Green Hill Far Away*  F(e-f), E(eb-e)

Howell, *By the Waters of Babylon*  G(B-G), Eb(G-eb)

Lehmann, *No Candle was There and No Fire*  Eb(eb-G), C(C-e)
Liddle, *An Old French Carol*  F(f-f), Db(db-db)
Liddle, *How Lovely Are Thy Dwellings*  Eb(eb-Ab), Db(db-Gb), C(C-f), Bb(Bb-eb)
Liddle, *The Lord is My Shepherd*  F(e-f), Eb(d-eb), D(C#-d), C(B-c)

MacDermid, *The Ninety-First Psalm*  Gb(eb-Ab)
Malotte, *The Lord's Prayer*  Eb(eb-Ab), Db(db-Gb), Bb(Bb-eb)
Martin, *The Holy Child*  C(g-G), Bb(f-f), Ab(eb-eb)

Neidlinger, *The Birthday of a King*  Bb(C-G), Ab(Bb-f)
Nevin, *Jesu, Jesu Miserere*  F(e-f), Eb(d-eb)

Riego, del, *O Loving Father*  Ab(f-Ab), F(d-f), Db(Bb-db)

Scott, *Come Ye Blessed*  Ab(eb-Ab), F(C-f), Eb(Bb-eb)
Seaver, *Just for Today*  F(d-G), Eb(C-f), Db(Bb-eb)

# APPENDIX

Shepperd, *Immortality* Ab(eb-Ab), F(C-f), D(A-d)
Shepperd, *Lead Kindly Light* C(d#-G), A(B#-e)

VandeWater, *The Good Shepherd* F(C-G), D(A-e)

West, *It Came Upon the Midnight Clear* E(e-f#), D(d-e)
West, *That Sweet Story of Old* Gb(gb-Gb), Bb(Bb-bb)

Yon, *Jesu, Bambino* G(d-G), Eb(Bb-eb)

## MIXED VOICES
### (S A T B)

Arne, *The Lass With the Delicate Air*
Arnold, *Lolita*

Bach, *Break Forth, O Beauteous Heavenly Light*
Bach, *Jesu, Joy of Man's Desiring*
Bach, *Jesu, Priceless Treasure*
Baini, *Panis Angelicus*
Burney, *Alla Trinita*

Clokey, *Kye Song of Saint Bride*
Cowen, *Bridal Chorus* from "Rose Maiden"

Elgar, *My Love Dwelt in a Northern Land*
English Folk Song, *The Keeper*

Finnish Folk Song, *The Lovely Rose*
Foster, *Jeanie with the Light Brown Hair*
French Carol of the 15th Century, *Sing Noël*

Gounod, *Chorus of Revelers* from "Philemon and Baucis"
Gounod, *Waltz* from "Faust"

Molloy, *The Kerry Dance*
Morley, *April is in My Mistress' Face*
Morley, *My Bonnie Lass She Smileth*

Negro Spiritual, *My Lord, What a Morning*

Pilkington, *Downe-a-Downe*

Roberton, *All in the April Evening*
Russian Folk Dance, *Little Duck in the Meadow*

Schuetky, *Emitte Spiritum*
Slovak Folk Song, *Come You Here, Laddie*

Wilson, *In the Merry Month of May*

## MALE VOICES
### (T T B B)

Andrews, *Sea Fever*

Bantock, *Down Among the Dead Men*
Bartholomew, *Hooda Dey*
Bartholomew, *Shenandoah*
Bartholomew, *Three Negro Spirituals*
Bartholomew, *Three Sea Chanteys*
Bullard, *Winter Song*

Cadman, *The Builders*
Chudleigh-Candish, *Song of the Jolly Roger*
Clay, *Gypsy John*
Clough-Leighter, *My Lady Chloe*

English Ballad, *John Peel*

Foote, *Bedouin Love Song*

German, *Rolling Down to Rio*
Gounod, *Soldiers' Chorus* from "Faust"
Grieg, *Landsighting*

Kountz, *A-Hunting We Will Go*

Nevin, *Song of the Armourer*

Parker, *Lamp in the West*
Parks, *Pale in the Amber West*
Pinsuti, *Good Night, Beloved*
Protheroe, *Shadow March*
Protheroe, *Song of the Road*
Protheroe, *Song of the Western Men*

Robinson, *Water Boy*

Schumann, *The Peaceful Lake*
Scotch Song, *Loch Lomond*
Scotch Song, *Ye Banks and Braes*

Terry, *Sailor Chanties*

Wolfe, *Shortnin' Bread*

# ADDITIONAL LIST OF SONGS

## TREBLE VOICES
### (S S A)

Andrews, *Pierrot*

Brewer, *Fairy Pipers*

Calcott, *How Sweet the Moonlight*
Cook, *Within a Dreaming Harbor*
Cox, *The Shepherdess*

Daniels, *June Rhapsody*
Davis, *The Cobbler's Jig*

Elgar, *The Snow*
English Folk Song, *Day at the Fair*

Foster, *Come Where My Love Lies Dreaming*

Grieg, *In the Boat*

Handel, *Let Us Wander*
Harris, *Ghosts*
Hildach, *The Minstrel*

Irish Melody, *The Galway Piper*
Irish Melody, *Would God I Were the Tender Apple Blossom*

Kreisler, *Cradle Song*

Matthews, *Persian Serenade*

Nevin, *Mighty Lak' a Rose*
Nevin, *The Woodpecker*
Newton, *Madrigal in May*

Parker, *In Maytime* (*S S A A*)

Roberton, *Celtic Lullaby*

Speaks, *Morning*
Speaks, *To You*

Taylor, *My Johnny Was a Shoemaker*
Taylor, *Twenty-Eighteen*

## TREBLE VOICES
### (S A)

Adams, *Cantique de Noël*
Ambrose, *One Sweetly Solemn Thought*

Bach, *Hey Derry, Down Derry*
Brahms, *Birth of Joy*

Calver, *Who Has Seen the Wind*
Chilean Folk Song, *River, River*

Edwards, *By the Bend of the River*
English Melody (arr. with descant) *The Banks of Allan Water*

French Carol, *Bring a Torch, Jeannette, Isabella*

Lithuanian Folk Song, *The Children's Prayer*

Mendelssohn, *I Would That My Love*

Negro Spiritual, *Deep River*

Negro Spiritual, *Heav'n, Heav'n*

Offenbach, *Barcarolle* from "Tales of Hoffman"

Pinsuti, *When Life is Brightest*
Polish Folk Song, *Star Lullaby*

Rachmaninoff, *The Lonely Pine*
Ries, *Cradle Song*
Rubinstein, *The Angel*

Schubert, *Who is Sylvia?*
Scotch Folk Song (arr. with descant) *Will Ye No Come Back Again?*
Smart, *The Lord is My Shepherd*

Terry, *Sailor Chanties* (arr. with descant)
Tosti, *Serenade*

Wilson, *Carmena Waltz*

# C. GLOSSARY [1]

*A Cappella*, In "chapel style"; unaccompanied.

*A tempo*, in regular time.

*Accelerando*, increasing the rate of speed.

*Ad libitum*, at will; as one wishes.

*Adagio*, slow.

*Allargando*, gradually slower.

*Allegretto*, moderately fast; a little slower than *allegro*.

*Allegro*, fast.

*Andante*, moderately slow.

*Andantino*, diminutive of *andante*, therefore slightly faster than *andante*.

*Animato*, with spirit.

*Aria*, a term commonly applied to songs in opera or oratorio.

*Arpeggio*, derived from the Italian words *arpa* meaning "harp" and *arpeggiare* "to play on the harp"; therefore, in the style of harp playing. The employment in vocal or instrumental music of notes of a chord in succession instead of simultaneously.

*Art Song*, a song in which the music reflects and interprets the meaning of the poem throughout and is not merely repeated for successive stanzas as in the strophic song. Sometimes called a "through composed" song.

*Assai*, very; very much.

*Ballad*, a song, the words of which tell a story. The term is also applied to songs having popular appeal.

*Baritone* (*Barytone*), the male voice lying between the tenor and bass in quality and range.

*Bass* (*Basso*), the heaviest in quality and usually the lowest in range of male voices. The term is derived from the French word "*bas*" meaning "low."

*Bel canto*, literally "beautiful singing"; the art of smooth, flowing singing.

*Brio*, vigor.

*Cadence*, the ending or last tones of a musical phrase, section, movement, or complete composition.

*Cantabile*, in singing style.

*Cantante*, singing.

*Con*, with.

*Contralto*, the heaviest in quality and usually the lowest in range of women's voices.

*Crescendo* (cresc., ⟨⟩), gradually growing louder.

*Coloratura soprano*, a voice of high range and of great natural flexibility capable of brilliant effects.

*Da Capo*, literally "from the head," *i.e.*, repeat from the beginning.

*Dal Segno* (D.S.) indicates a repetition from the sign ( 𝄋 or ◆ ).

*Decrescendo* (decresc., ⟩), gradually decreasing the volume of tone.

*Di*, of.

*Diminuendo* (dim.), same as *decrescendo*.

*Dolce*, sweetly, tenderly.

---

[1] This list of musical terms is by no means complete, but does include those commonly used. For a more exhaustive list see a standard dictionary of music.

# GLOSSARY

*Dramatic*, used with voices, as *dramatic tenor* or *dramatic soprano*. It denotes voices appropriate for use in dramatic music. In contrast to lyric it signifies a heavier, more intense quality.

*Dynamics*, refers to various degrees of power of tones, *i.e.*, comparative loudness and softness.

*Energico*, energy, force.
*Espressione*, expression.

*Fermata* (⌒) hold.
*Fine*, the end.
*Folk Song*, a song of simple structure, the source of which is unknown. Some definitions include a song of similar type by a known composer which expresses some deep emotion of a people and which has become a traditional part of their melodic literature.
*Forte* (f), loud.
*Fortissimo* (ff), very loud.
*Forzando*, (sfz) strongly accented.

*Giocoso*, merrily.
*Grave*, gravely, solemnly.
*Grazia*, gracefully.

*Largamente*, in broad style.
*Largo*, slow and broad in style.
*Legato*, connected and smooth.
*Lento*, very slow.
*Lunga*, long.
*Lyric*, a short, song-like poem; a song which is personal in its expression and is thus concerned with various phases of some emotional reaction to given situations; the opposite of *dramatic* songs which deal with events; used in connection with voices, as *lyric tenor* or *lyric soprano*, it denotes a flexible voice of light texture well suited to singing songs of a lyric type.

*Ma*, but.
*Madrigal*, (from the medieval Latin word *matricale* meaning a rustic song), a secular composition usually having from three to eight parts and written in rather elaborate contrapuntal style. Madrigals were first developed in the sixteenth century. After about 1625 they were supplanted by other vocal forms.
*Marcato*, marked.
*Meno*, less.
*Mezzo*, half; medium.
*Mezzo soprano*, the woman's voice between the soprano and contralto in quality and range.
*Molto*, much.
*Morendo*, dying away.
*Mosso*, literally "move," motion, faster.

*Non*, no.
*Nuance*, delicate shading.

*Opera*, a composition for vocal soloists, chorus, and orchestra with scenery and dramatic movement: a drama set to music.

# APPENDIX

*Oratorio*, a composition for soloists, chorus, and orchestra, the text of a religious or heroic nature intended for presentation without action or scenery.

*Ossia*, offering an alternative.

*Parlando*, speaking; in declamatory style.

*Pianissimo* (pp), very softly.

*Piano* (p), softly.

*Più*, more.

*Poco*, a little.

*Portamento*, with tone carried smoothly from one pitch to another.

*Prestissimo*, as fast as possible.

*Presto*, quickly.

*Profundo*, profound; deep.

*Rallentando*, gradually slower.

*Recitative*, vocal declamation without fixed rhythm or balanced phrases and usually without much accompaniment. A style of vocal solo common to operas, oratorios, and cantatas. The words are of first importance, both rhythm and tone progression being regulated by rhetorical rather than musical considerations.

*Ritardando*, growing slower.

*Rubato*, with freedom of tempo; with retardation and acceleration.

*Semplice*, simply.

*Sempre*, always.

*Senza*, without.

*Sforzando*, with force or emphasis.

*Smorzando*, dying away.

*Soprano*, highest and lightest of women's voices; the word comes from the Italian word *sopra* meaning "above."

*Sostenuto*, sustained.

*Staccato* (indicated by a dot above or below notes), detached; disconnected; the opposite of *legato*.

*Strophe*, term applied to a song in which the same melody is used for successive verses.

*Subito*, suddenly.

*Tempo*, time; rate of speed.

*Tenor*, lightest in quality and usually the highest in range of men's voices.

*Tenuto*, hold.

*Timbre*, characteristic quality of tone that distinguishes one voice or instrument from another.

*Tranquillo*, tranquil.

*Tristezza*, sadness.

*Troppo*, too.

*Vivace*, lively.

*Voce*, voice.

# ALPHABETIC INDEX TO SONGS

# INDEX TO EXCERPTS FROM SONGS

## (Alphabetic by title)

# INDEX

48